D0087682

The Grievance Process in Labor-Management Cooperation

The Grievance Process in Labor-Management Cooperation

MICHAEL J. DUANE

QUORUM BOOKS
Westport, Connecticut • London

Library of Congress Cataloging-in-Publication Data

Duane, Michael John.
The grievance process in labor-management cooperation / Michael J. Duane
p. cm.
Includes bibliographical references (p.) and index.
ISBN 0–89930–760–4 (alk. paper)
1. Grievance procedures—United States. 2. Grievance arbitration—United States. 3. Industrial management—United States—Employee participation. 4. Industrial relations—United States. I. Title.
HD6972.5.D83 1993
331.88'96—dc20 92–44683

British Library Cataloguing in Publication Data is available.

Library of Congress Catalog Card Number: 92–44683
ISBN: 0–89930–760–4

First published in 1993

Quorum Books, 88 Post Road West, Westport, CT 06881
An imprint of Greenwood Publishing Group, Inc.

Printed in the United States of America

The paper used in this book complies with the Permanent Paper Standard issued by the National Information Standards Organization (Z39.48–1984).

10 9 8 7 6 5 4 3 2 1

Contents

Tables and Figures xi

1 Labor-Management Cooperation 1

The Labor-Management Relations Model 7

Conclusions 11

2 Joint Labor-Management Programs 13

Gainsharing Programs 15

Scanlon Program 16

Rucker Program 18

Improshare Program 20

Research on Gainsharing Programs 21

Nongainsharing Programs 23

Quality Circles 23

Labor-Management Committees 26

Research on Nongainsharing Programs 28

Appropriate Structure of Joint Labor-Management Programs 30

Conclusions 32

3 Contract Negotiations 35

Recent History of Labor-Management Relations 35

Union Avoidance 39

Decentralization of Bargaining 40

Changing Role of the Industrial Relations Staff 42

New Communications Policies 43

Strikebreaking Activities 44

Profile of a Union Avoider 45

Labor Movement's Response to Union Avoidance 46

Labor-Management Cooperation 52

Controlling Issues 53

Establishing and Maintaining Integrative Frameworks 55

Conclusions 60

4 The Grievance Process 63

The Standard Grievance Procedure 63

First Step 64

Second Step 65

Third Step 66

Fourth Step: Arbitration 66

Variations in Grievance Procedures 68

Agriculture, Construction, and Trucking Procedures 68

Public-Sector Procedures 69

Nonunion Procedures 70

International Procedures 72

The Grievance Process and Firm Performance 74

Employee Turnover 75

Strike Activity 77

Productivity 78

The Grievance Process and Joint Labor-Management Programs 81

The Grievance Process and Contract Negotiations 81

Interpreting Grievance Data 82

Grievance Rates 82

Settlement Level 84

Conclusions 85

5 The Impact of Background and Boundary-Role Factors on the Grievance Process 89

Background Factors 89

Personality 89

Negotiating Experience 91

Education 92

Gender 93

Race 94

Marital Status 94

Summary of the Effects of Background Factors 95

Boundary-Role Factors 95

Constituent Demands 96

The Grievance Officials' Relationship 103

Summary of the Effects of Boundary-Role Factors 108

6 The Impact of Environmental Factors on the Grievance Process 109

Economic Conditions 109

Technology 111

Legal Regulations 114

Bargaining Setting 121

The Collective Bargaining Agreement 123

Conclusions 125

7 Implications and Conclusions 127

Implications of the Labor-Management Relations Model 127

Improving the Grievance Process 129

Selection Programs 129

Training Programs 130

Performance Appraisal 132

Reward System 133
Concluding Comments 134
References 135
Name Index 149
Subject Index 155

Tables and Figures

Tables

1.1 Inducement-to-Agree Ratios 3

1.2 Potential Costs and Benefits of Labor-Management Cooperation 6

2.1 Comparison of Gainsharing Programs 14

2.2 Scanlon Plan Example 17

2.3 Rucker Plan Example 19

2.4 Improshare Plan Example 22

2.5 Comparison of Nongainsharing Programs 24

2.6 Characteristics of Quality Circles 26

3.1 Union-Avoidance Strategy: Management's Tactics 41

3.2 Union-Avoidance Strategy: Union's Roles 47

3.3 Techniques for Depersonalizing the Bargaining Process 56

4.1 Representative Grievance Procedure 65

4.2 European Grievance Procedures 72

4.3 Summary of Propositions on the Relationship Between the Grievance Process and Labor-Management Outcomes 86

5.1 Summary of Propositions on the Effects of Background Factors 96

5.2 Summary of Propositions on the Effects of Boundary-Role Factors 106

6.1 Summary of Propositions on the Effects of Environmental Factors 124

Figures

1.1 Labor-Management Relations Model 9

4.1 Grievance Rate and Productivity 79

The Grievance Process in Labor-Management Cooperation

1

Labor-Management Cooperation

Labor-management cooperation has become an integral part of what Kochan, Katz, and McKersie (1986) call the "transformation of American industrial relations." Responding to this observation, Chelius and Dworkin (1990, p. 1) note that during the 1980s "many aspects of the relationship between employers and employees have changed substantially. In numerous settings there has been an increase in the level of employee participation, with the focus ranging from limited workplace issues to broad strategic aspects of business operations." But, since it is generally assumed that the principles by which management and unionized workers operate are not only different, but conflicting, why would these parties even entertain the idea of cooperating with each other? A fundamental understanding of bargaining theory will provide some insight into this issue.

Within the traditional collective bargaining relationship, labor and management attempt to achieve their individual objectives by exercising their relative bargaining power. As president of the American Federation of Labor (AFL), William Green popularized the phrase *bargaining power* by repeatedly referring to it in his testimony before the Senate Education and Labor Committee in

1935. Since then, several scholars have offered definitions of it. The following are two representative examples:

> [Bargaining] power is defined as the capacity of one subject to carry through its will against the will of another subject (Pen, 1952, p. 24).
>
> Bargaining power can be defined as the capacity to effect an agreement on one's own terms (Chamberlain, 1955, p. 80).

While these definitions differ in terms of their element of coercion, with the second one somewhat more compassionate, both of them implicitly stress the concept of inducement. To illustrate, when management (union) makes an offer to settle on certain terms, union's (management's) inducement-to-agree ratio is defined as the cost of disagreeing on management's (union's) terms divided by the cost of agreeing on management's (union's) terms (see Table 1.1). According to Reynolds, Masters, and Moser (1986), an inducement-to-agree ratio will usually be greater than zero, but not necessarily greater than one. They note that only if and when it becomes greater than one—that is, when the cost of continued disagreement exceeds the cost of agreement—will management (union) be willing to accept union's (management's) offer.

The value of an opponent's inducement-to-agree ratio can be raised, eventually bringing about a settlement, by either decreasing that side's cost of agreeing or by increasing their cost of disagreement. For example, assume that after several weeks of heated contract negotiations, a union eventually lowers its wage demand in order to avoid a threatened employee lockout; in effect, the union has decreased management's cost of agreement by making wage concessions, thereby, all things equal, raising management's inducement-to-agree ratio. From management's perspective, on the other hand, the threatened lockout was effectively used to increase the union's cost of not making such concessions. As this example suggests, bargaining power is the primary tool that a party uses to raise the other side's inducement-to-agree ratio. Indeed,

Table 1.1
Inducement-to-Agree Ratios

$$\text{Union's Inducement-to-Agree Ratio} = \frac{\text{Union's Cost of Disagreeing with Management}}{\text{Union's Cost of Agreeing with Management}}$$

$$\text{Management's Inducement-to-Agree Ratio} = \frac{\text{Management's Cost of Disagreeing with the Union}}{\text{Management's Cost of Agreeing with the Union}}$$

Source: Equations are modified slightly from F. Ray Marshall and Vernon M. Briggs, Labor Economics (6th ed.). (Homewood, IL: Richard D. Irwin, 1989), p. 247.

even though the union is willing to make some wage adjustments, presumably there is a wage level (resistance point) at which the union would elect to strike, or in this case to suffer a lockout, rather than settle. When these intentions are convincingly conveyed to management, they increase management's cost of not offering an acceptable wage.

The inducement process reveals that relative bargaining power is so elusive that a skillful negotiator may change it by relying on different tactics to alter perceived or actual costs of agreement or disagreement. Negotiating skill, however, is only part of the equation. In point of fact, a union's threat to strike over a particular wage demand will be met with greater management resistance when the firm is undergoing financial difficulties. Moreover, government interventions have a tremendous effect on the negotiation process generally and on the parties' relative bargaining powers in particular. In the public sector, for instance, unions have limited access to the strike as a tool of persuasion, thus decreasing their relative bargaining powers. Chamberlain and Kuhn (1986) also note that public opinion, technology, and ability to suffer a lockout or strike have significant implications for each side's bargaining strength.

In short, the conventional view of bargaining power is that those who have more of it have the ability to beat their opponents, where the aim is to increase one's net gain at the other's expense. Obviously, the history of labor-management relations is fraught with cases where individual parties have realized substantial benefits by flexing their bargaining muscle. Recent evidence, however, reveals that over time these gains may diminish to a point where future gains from using this adversarial approach are expected to be negligible, at best. And it is at this point that the parties may examine other options to achieve their goals, including labor-management cooperation.

It is no secret that many managers and union leaders alike will always treat the labor-management relationship as adversarial, with inherent conflicts of interest. Where there is this lack of good faith, cooperation is not possible. On the other hand, when the parties have come to believe that they have more to gain, or less to lose, from joint efforts than from the continued use of individual bargaining power, cooperation may emerge as a possible direction for future interactions, both within their conventional activities, consisting of contract and grievance negotiations, as well as outside of them, including joint labor-management programs (e.g., Scanlon programs and quality circles). A number of instances of labor-management cooperation have, in fact, developed out of a crisis for survival of the firm. As Bok and Dunlop (1970, p. 266) note, the "threat of a plant shutdown or a loss of jobs has led the parties to join in trying to improve the competitive position of the enterprise." And developments since these remarks were made, particularly in the global arena, have only intensified the need for cooperation.

Management and organized labor have also embarked on cooperative efforts under less pressing circumstances. Surveys conducted by the Work in America Institute (1982), Cooke (1990), Kochan, McKersie, and Chalykoff (1986), and the U.S. Department of Labor (1990) reveal that approximately half of the unionized organizations in the United States have implemented joint labor-management programs for a variety of reasons, ranging from an attempt to enhance communication between the parties to an overall effort to improve productivity and product quality. While joint labor-management action may offer potential benefits to the parties, it also is likely to involve potential costs. Table 1.2 presents some expected outcomes from labor-management cooperation.

The potential benefits to management from joint action with organized labor include a decline in costs of production and an increase in product quality, which, in either case, ensures greater competitive advantage for the firm. In particular, a reduction in production costs is likely to occur out of programs associated with a more efficient use of materials, a decline in accident and error rates, or an increase in output per unit of labor. Product quality, on the other hand, may be enhanced by programs aimed at quality control, innovation, and customer concerns.

For management, the downside of cooperation involves both pecuniary and nonpecuniary costs. With regard to the former, Cooke (1990, p. 8) notes that organizational "shifts from traditional and generally adversarial collective bargaining relationships and autocratic management practices . . . sometimes require sizable resources for reorientation and training of managers, supervisors, rank-and-file, and union representatives." Individual managers may also be anxious about loss of authority and, conceivably, loss of jobs stemming from cooperative ventures. This will be particularly true of first-line supervisors who are closest to rank-and-file workers, and who have in a sense become their equals in the parties' evolving relationship.

The major union benefits from labor-management cooperation focus on employee gains, including greater job security, improved working conditions, and better communication with management. Moreover, assuming that joint activities result in these benefits, union officials may gain greater respect from their constituencies. Cooperation, as noted earlier, is also likely to improve the overall relationship between the union and management, possibly opening up other avenues of mutually benefiting interactions.

Table 1.2
Potential Costs and Benefits of Labor-Management Cooperation

MANAGEMENT

Potential Benefits	Potential Costs
1. Increased productivity and efficiency	1. Added training costs associated with the programs
2. Improved quality of product and service	2. Perceived loss of authority and status
3. Improved customer relations	3. Displacement or loss of jobs for managers
4. Reduced waste and rework	4. Wasted time spent in meetings
5. Reduced overhead and other related costs	
6. Improved communication	
7. Improved relationships between supervisors and employees	
8. Reduced grievances and disciplinary action	
9. Reduced absenteeism, tardiness, and turnover	
10. Stronger commitment to organizational goals	

A conceivable cost to the union consists of membership perception that union officials have become too friendly with management. Indeed, the union and management must be cautious in their collaborative activities, since the National Labor Relations Act (NLRA) along with other state and local labor laws prohibit "puppet" or company unions whose interests really lie with management rather than with their members. The most significant disincentive for union officials to cooperate with management, however, is the potential loss of membership support, as employees become more trusting of management and committed to organizational goals. And to this end, the traditional roles of unions and collective bargaining are undermined. Speaking to this concern, Chamberlain and Kuhn (1986, p. 461) observe that "if harmony of

Table 1.2 (Continued)

UNION

Potential Benefits	Potential Costs
1. Recognition from members for improvements	1. Perceived cooptation by management
2. Greater participation in management decisions	2. Displacement or loss of employment for members
3. Improved communications with management	3. Loss of member support for the union or its leadership
4. Reduced contract administration problems	4. Unwanted peer pressure to be involved or not involved
	5. Undermining traditional roles of unions and collective bargaining
	6. Heightened political conflict over leadership role

Source: Concepts abstracted from William N. Cooke, Labor-Management Cooperation (Kalamazoo, MI: W. E. Upjohn Institute for Employment Research, 1990).

interest between employees and employer can be stressed and if managers are careful to give employees some share in the benefits of harmony . . . will not this rob union members of their militancy and even their desire to maintain a separate organization responsive to their peculiar interests?"

One conclusion that can be drawn from this discussion is that for the parties to fully realize the benefits from working together, they must address those facets of their relationship that promote genuine cooperation. In what follows, a model is proposed that will assist them in this analysis.

THE LABOR-MANAGEMENT RELATIONS MODEL

The literature is rich with cost-benefit analyses of cooperative labor-management programs that lie outside the traditional bargaining relationship (Cooke, 1990; Havlovic, 1991; Schuster, 1984b; Voos, 1989) as well as those associated with cooperative contract negotiations (Crisci, 1986; Kuhns, 1986; Schachter, 1989). To date, however, there has not been a thorough examination of the role of the grievance process in labor-management cooperative ventures. This is particularly disturbing since Freeman and Medoff (1984), Katz, Kochan, and Gobeille (1983), and Ichniowski (1986) note that the state of labor-management relations, as defined by grievance activity at the shop level, determines to a large degree whether such ventures will be productive. It is this premise that provides the foundation for a theoretical model that incorporates the effects of the grievance process on labor-management relations.

The Labor-Management Relations (LMR) model (see Figure 1.1), consists of seven components: boundary-role factors, background factors, environmental factors, grievance process, joint labor-management programs, contract negotiations, and labor-management outcomes. In the remainder of this chapter, each of these components is briefly discussed, with the exception of labor-management outcomes, which have already been introduced.

The LMR model assumes that interactions between labor and management can be characterized as falling along a continuum that ranges from adversarial or uncooperative, where at least one of the parties takes a strong competitive stance against the other; to cooperative, which involves an attempt to work with the other side in the hope of achieving mutually satisfying solutions to problems. An adversarial stance is routinely adopted by those parties who view collective bargaining as a win-lose confrontation, where bargaining power dominates. Parties that elect to engage in cooperation, on the other hand, view their relationship from a win-win perspective, where the goal is, according to Cross (1969) and Chamberlain and Kuhn (1986), not to impose unfavorable, costly terms on the other, but to set the terms for future, ongoing productive interactions.

At the heart of the model is the grievance process. As with other terms and conditions of employment, a *grievance* is defined by the

Figure 1.1
Labor-Management Relations Model

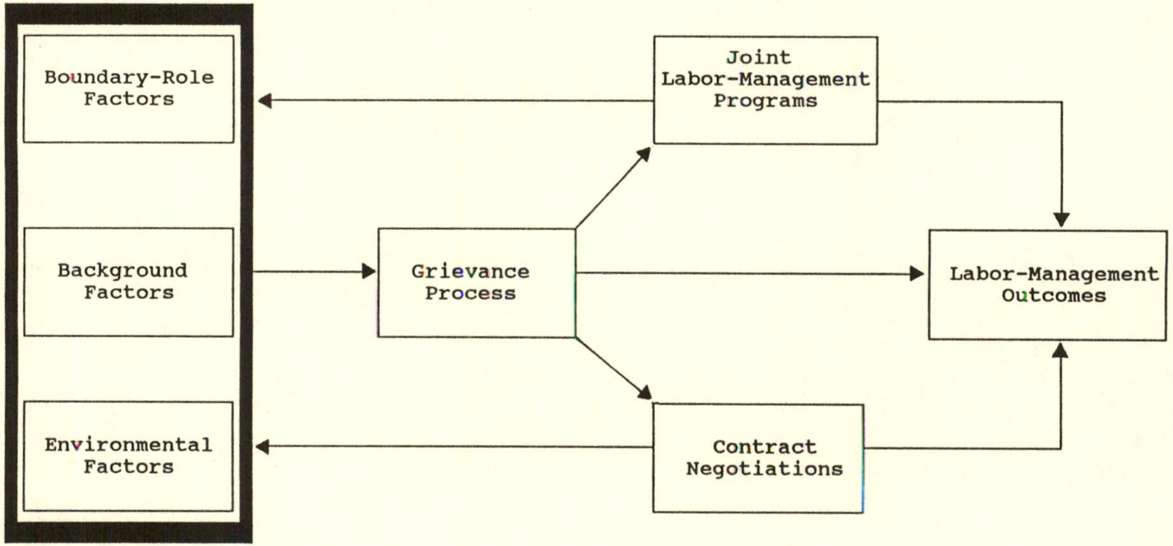

Boundary-Role Factors

Background Factors

Environmental Factors

Grievance Process

Joint Labor-Management Programs

Contract Negotiations

Labor-Management Outcomes

parties through collective bargaining, and thus, provided that it complies with the appropriate legal constraints, it can be anything that they want it to be. In general, however, a grievance is a written allegation by the union that management has in some way misinterpreted the terms of the collective bargaining agreement when administering it. Accordingly, officials from each side attempt to resolve the dispute through discussion and negotiation. As the model illustrates, there are three categories of factors that account for a grievance official's level of cooperation during such deliberations: boundary-role factors, background factors, and environmental factors.

The boundary-role factors involve representative functions that at first glance appear to be at odds with each other. Specifically, the grievance officials represent their groups' positions and interests to the other side; hence, their bargaining orientations will be influenced by constituent demands and expectations. But they also represent the views of the other side to their constituents, and in doing so, the officials are likely to be familiar with the other side's priorities, strengths, weaknesses, and predilections. With this special knowledge, they are bound to alter how they approach the resolution of grievances.

The literature on bargaining behavior also suggests that an official's approach to resolving grievances is likely to be influenced by several background factors: personality, education, negotiating experience, gender, race, and marital status. Added to these factors are the effects of the bargaining environment, which consists of economic conditions, technology, legal regulations, bargaining setting, and the collective bargaining agreement.

Following the prescribed causal relationship, the model indicates that the grievance process, particularly the manner in which union and management officials resolve worker complaints, influences other aspects of the parties' relationship. In particular, a cooperative (adversarial) grievance orientation tends to foster cooperative (adversarial) contract negotiations. Moreover, the degree of cooperation (adversity) on joint projects is likely to be affected by the way the parties resolve their day-to-day worker complaints and concerns.

Finally, the model prescribes that while the grievance process directly affects certain labor-management outcomes as well as the character of the parties' contract negotiations and joint projects, it is indirectly influenced by them, since they are expected to interact with the grievance officials' boundary-role and environmental factors. To illustrate, with the introduction of a joint labor-management program, union and management grievance officials will have more of an opportunity to interact, which is likely to result in a better understanding of each other's true intentions and predispositions. This additional information, in turn, will alter how they approach their boundary-roles. Similarly, an important by-product of contract negotiations is the bargaining agreement itself. Research suggests that when the provisions of the agreement are negotiated cooperatively, they tend to be clearer and more specific than if they had been determined through the exclusive use of relative bargaining power. For the grievance officials, who are responsible for administering and interpreting the contract on a daily basis, clear and specific provisions promote cooperation to the extent that there is little need to haggle over vague understanding.

CONCLUSIONS

The remainder of the book examines more thoroughly the components of the LMR model. In particular, Chapter 2 addresses joint labor-management programs. Chapter 3 discusses contract negotiations, with an emphasis on how they have been affected by recent developments in labor-management relations. It also presents recommendations on how to foster cooperation at the bargaining table. Chapter 4 examines the grievance process. It begins by reviewing the various types of grievance procedures. The relationship between the grievance process and labor-management outcomes is also investigated. Moreover, the implications of using grievance data in describing labor-management relations are addressed. Chapter 5 discusses the effects of background and boundary-role factors on the bargaining behaviors of grievance officials. Chapter 6 examines how the bargaining environment affects the behaviors of grievance officials. Finally, Chapter 7 discusses some of the model's indirect effects. It also presents some conclusions from the model and recommendations on how to improve the grievance process.

2

Joint Labor-Management Programs

The potential for cooperation between management and labor is not restricted to conventional collective bargaining activities. In a recent U.S. Department of Labor study (1990), for example, over half of the joint labor-management programs cited did not involve collective bargaining relationships. That is, several programs that involved organized labor excluded contractual issues from consideration. Other programs did not involve union participation at all, either because the unions chose not to take part or because the firms were nonunionized. Commenting on the difference between union and nonunion programs, Verma and McKersie (1987) assert that when the union participates, the employees perceive the shared decision-making process to be more legitimate, believing that their interests will be protected. They suggest, therefore, that employee commitment to labor-management cooperative programs and to the implementation of their outcomes may be strengthened by union involvement.

At the cost of oversimplification, it can be argued that labor-management cooperative programs differ in terms of whether or not they include gainsharing intervention. Gainsharing programs combine employee participation with a financial formula for dis-

Table 2.1
Comparison of Gainsharing Programs

Dimension	Scanlon	Rucker	Improshare
Philosophy	Org-single unit; share improvements; people capable/willing to make suggestions, want to make ideas	Primarily economic incentive; some reliance on employee participation	Economic incentives increase performance
Primary goal	Productivity improvement	Productivity improvement	Productivity improvement
Subsidiary goals	Attitudes, communication, work behaviors, quality, cost reduction	Attitudes, communication, work behaviors, quality, cost reductions	Attitudes, work behaviors
Worker participation	Two levels of committees: screening (1), production (many)	Screening (1), production (1) (sometimes)	Bonus committee
Suggestion making	Formal system	Formal system	None

tributing economic benefits that are the results of improved organizational performance (Bullock & Lawler, 1984; Hammer, 1988; Lawler, 1986). While profit sharing is often considered a special case of gainsharing, there are some important differences between them. First, gainsharing rewards are typically tied to a measure of productivity, which workers have some control over, rather than to a measure of global profitability. Second, the distribution of rewards to workers under gainsharing generally occurs on a monthly or quarterly basis, rather than annually, which is common for profit sharing. Finally, gainsharing is a current distribution system, while profit sharing often incorporates deferred rewards to be paid out when vested workers leave the organization.

In sum, gainsharing operates closer to the workers, making it clearer to them the relationship between "their effort, the im-

Table 2.1 (Continued)

Dimension	Scanlon	Rucker	Improshare
Role of supervisor	Chair, production committee	None	None
Role of managers	Direct participation in bonus committee assignments	Idea coordinator evaluates suggestions, committee assignments	None
Bonus formula	Sales / payroll	Bargaining unit payroll / Production value	Engineered std. x BPF / Total hours worked
Frequency of payout	Monthly	Monthly	Weekly
Role of union	Negotiated provisions, screening committee membership	Negotiated provisions, screening committee membership	Negotiated provisions
Impact on management style	Substantial	Slight	None

Source: Michael Schuster, Union-Management Cooperation: Structure, Process, and Impact (Kalamazoo, MI: W. E. Upjohn Institute for Employment Research, 1984), pp. 76-77.

provements in productivity, and their personal outcomes" (Hammer, 1988, p. 335). Not surprisingly, therefore, research overwhelming indicates that mainstream gainsharing is more effective than profit sharing in generating desired labor-management outcomes (Heneman, Schwab, Fossum, & Dyer, 1989; Lawler, 1986; Sherman & Bohlander, 1992). For this reason, profit sharing will not be considered further. In what follows, specific gainsharing and nongainsharing programs are examined.

GAINSHARING PROGRAMS

As Table 2.1 indicates, there are a variety of gainsharing options: Scanlon, Rucker, and Improshare. While the primary goal of each of these intervention techniques is to improve productivity, their individual structures vary somewhat.

Scanlon Program

The philosophy of the Scanlon program, named after Joseph Scanlon, president of a local union during the mid-1930s, is that workers are willing to offer their talents, ideas, and suggestions to improve organizational performance, provided that management rewards them for these inputs. Out of this philosophy flows a structure that supports a very elaborate method of employee participation. In brief, at the foundation of most Scanlon programs is an employee-suggestion system that addresses plant operations. Review of these suggestions begins with one of several production committees located throughout a plant. These committees typically consist of two to five rank-and-file workers elected by their peers, as well as a supervisor or foreman. Other functions of the production committees are to implement those suggestions deemed to have merit, given that they fall within the committee's jurisdiction and within specified cost limits. They also make recommendations to a screening committee concerning suggestions that may have broader organizational ramifications.

Members of the screening committee include rank-and-file workers and key executives, usually plant or divisional managers. According to Schuster (1984b, p. 85), some of the primary responsibilities of the screening committee include:

> First, suggestions which cross the boundaries of production committees or exceed the cost guidelines of a production committee must be approved by the screening committee. Second, . . . suggestions rejected by the production committees can be appealed to the screening committee. Third, it insures that issues or items raised by the production and screening committees coming within the scope of the collective bargaining agreement, may not be discussed in those forums. Fourth, the screening committee considers current

Table 2.2
Scanlon Plan Example

Sales value of production	$70,000
Expected labor costs	$45,000
Actual labor costs	- $35,000
Bonus pool	$10,000
Reserve (25%)	- $ 2,500
Available bonus distribution	$ 7,500
Company share (25%)	- $ 1,857
Employees share (75%)	$ 5,643

Source: Modified by permission from (p. 316) of Productivity Through People by William B. Werther, William Ruch, and Lynne McClure;

and future business problems, as well as other issues of organizational concern (for example, production difficulties and customer complaints). Fifth, the screening committee reviews the monthly bonus calculations.

While suggestions may originate from individual employees, distribution of bonuses among co-workers is intended to create a cohesive work group environment that not only strengthens commitment to common goals, but also encourages individual creativity. The standard Scanlon-program formula is based on three central variables: sales value of production; expected labor costs, estimated from previous production periods; and actual labor costs for the period in question. Suppose, for example, that a small manufacturing firm's expected monthly labor costs is $45,000. Now, assume that the sales value of production for a particular month is $70,000 and that, due to the implementation of a Scanlon cost-savings suggestion, the actual labor costs for the month are $35,000 (see Table 2.2). The $10,000 savings are shared with employees, who generally receive about 50 to 75 percent of them, with the balance going to the firm.

Most Scanlon programs also establish a reserve in order to safeguard against possible negative results that may not be attributable to employee performance. If, at the end of the year, funds remain in this account, they are distributed using the same employee-company split.

Rucker Program

As Table 2.1 illustrates, the Rucker program, developed by the economist Allen Rucker in the 1930s, contains many of the same constructs found in the Scanlon program. There are, however, several differences. First, the Rucker program places less emphasis on employee participation. Many Rucker variations, for example, include only a screening committee composed of rank-and-file workers, selected by management and/or the union; a union official; and key management personnel. The primary functions of this committee consist of discussing productivity and product quality issues, reviewing employee suggestions for improvements in these areas, and supervising the bonus program.

In those instances where the program embodies lower-level involvement, the screening committee is often paired up with only one production committee, compared with several under the Scanlon system. When a production committee is included, it usually consists of 10 to 15 employees and a number of low-level managers, and meets periodically (monthly or weekly), on company time, to discuss production problems and to review employee suggestions. But as Schuster (1984b) points out, the Rucker-type production committee tends to be used more as a means of communication rather than a genuine method of problem-solving. This gainsharing option, therefore, may be appropriate for those firms that are attempting to ease into a more participatory structure. Indeed, Sherman and Bohlander (1992, p. 370) note that the Rucker program "commonly represents a type of program that is used as an alternative to the Scanlon program in firms attempting to move from a traditional style of management toward a higher level of employee involvement."

Table 2.3
Rucker Plan Example

Past data indicate that the proportion of value added allotted to payroll costs is .40.

Thus, the Rucker standard = .40

Current month's sales value of production		$70,000
Raw materials and supplies	-	$ 5,000
Value added		$65,000
Rucker standard	x	.40
Allowed Payroll costs		$26,000
This month's payroll costs	-	$22,000
Bonus available		$ 4,000
Company share (50%)	-	$ 2,000
Employees' share (50%)		$ 2,000
Reserve (10%)	-	$ 200
Bonus		$ 1,800

Percentage share for each employee
(Bonus total/Actual month's payroll costs) 8.18%

Joe Smith's payroll record for this month might look like this:

Name	Monthly pay	Bonus %	Bonus	Total Pay
Joe Smith	$2,000	8.18%	$163.60	$2,163.60

Source: Modified by permission from (p. 317) of Productivity Through People by William B. Werther, William Ruch, and Lynne McClure;

Another important distinction between the Scanlon and Rucker programs is how benefits are calculated and distributed. The Rucker method of calculating bonuses is somewhat more complex—that is, its formula includes an estimate of the proportion of value added allotted to payroll costs, using several years of data (Werther, Ruch, & McClure, 1986). This estimate is often referred to as the Rucker standard. For any given month, the allowed payroll costs are computed by multiplying the Rucker standard by the month's value added, which is calculated by subtracting the costs of raw materials and supplies from sales value of production. The actual payroll costs are then subtracted from the resulting product to generate the bonus available. Table 2.3 provides an example of this calculation.

By incorporating the value-added component into the bonus calculation, the objective is to motivate employees to consider not only increased productivity, but also the costs of materials and supplies. Thus, less wasteful usage of these production inputs will, all things equal, result in greater employee bonuses. Finally, many Rucker programs distribute benefits on a percentage basis rather than by absolute dollar dispersement. The intent here is to encourage the higher paid employees, who usually have more seniority and experience, and who likely have greater knowledge of firm operations, to become actively involved in the program.

Improshare Program

Mitchell Fain, an industrial engineer, recently capitalized on the basic tenets of gainsharing with the introduction of Improshare or *improved productivity through sharing*. As Table 2.1 points out, Improshare allows the least amount of employee involvement among the three gainsharing options. Indeed, those Improshare programs studied by Schuster (1984b) did not endorse any model of formal employee participation, other than each worker's individual contribution to production efficiency.

Similar to the Scanlon program, Improshare measures only labor costs, but it also "uses engineered time standards to calculate a base productivity factor" (Hammer, 1988, p. 338). The Base Productivity Factor (BPF), which operates as a benchmark measure of productivity, makes it possible to include the contributions to productivity by nonproduction or indirect employees, such as clerical and other support staff, along with those made by the workers who are tied closer to the actual production process. The BPF is computed as follows:

$$\text{BPF} = \frac{\text{Total production and nonproduction hours}}{\text{Standard value hours}}$$

The total number of production and nonproduction hours is equal to the sum of hours worked by all group members. Total standard value hours are a function of the estimated time to produce a single unit, multiplied by total units produced during the period being evaluated. Table 2.4 provides a simple example of how the Improshare bonus is calculated. Under Improshare, gains in productivity are represented by the hours saved, with employees allotted half of them. These savings are then converted into an index that, when multiplied by an employee's gross pay, generates that person's bonus.

Research on Gainsharing Programs

Early research on gainsharing focused on Scanlon programs (for a detailed review of this research, see Schuster, 1983; Geare, 1976). While most of these studies are anecdotal accounts of gainsharing effects, they do generally show that these programs are associated with increased productivity and enhanced labor-management relations. These early assessments also suggest that such programs have a positive impact on worker attitudes and satisfaction.

Recent investigations of the effects of gainsharing programs have used *meta-analysis*. This methodology is a quantitative cumulation technique that allows researchers to gain a better understanding of a phenomenon by assessing the results across studies, rather than by relying on their individual results (for discussions of meta-analysis, see Cascio, 1991; Green & Hall, 1984; Rosnow & Rosenthal, 1989). To date, two meta-analyses of gainsharing programs have been performed. In one, Bullock and Lawler (1984) found that two-thirds of the studies showed improvements in productivity, product quality, cost reduction, worker attitudes, and quality of work life. Yet positive effects on labor-management relations and communication were observed in only half of the studies. In the other meta-analysis, Guzzo, Jette, and Katzell (1985) report that gainsharing programs, on average, increased productivity by 20 percent. There was, however, enormous variation among the studies, from a decrease of 5 percent in productivity to an increase as high as 75 percent. They suggest that the key to successful gainsharing is the careful fitting of incentive programs to workers, jobs, organizational structure, and other relevant factors.

Table 2.4
Improshare Plan Example

BASE PERIOD

10 employees worked 40 hours each to produce 1,000 units of product A.

Work hour standard (WHS) (product A):

$$\frac{(10 \text{ employees} \times 40 \text{ hours})}{1{,}000 \text{ units}} = 0.4 \text{ WHS}$$

15 employees worked 40 hours each to produce 500 units of product B.

WHS (product B):

$$\frac{(15 \text{ employees} \times 40 \text{ hours})}{500 \text{ units}} = 1.2 \text{ WHS}$$

Standard value hours (SVH):

Product A:	0.4 WHS x 1,000 units =	400 SVH
Product B:	1.2 WHS x 500 units =	600 SVH
Total		1,000 SVH

20 nonproduction employees worked 40 hours each.

(20 employees x 40 hours) = 800 nonproduction hours

Base Productivity Factor (BPF):

$$\text{BPF} = \frac{\text{Total production and nonproduction hours}}{\text{Total standard value hours}}$$

$$1.8 = \frac{[(10 \text{ employees} \times 40 \text{ hours}) + (15 \text{ employees} \times 40 \text{ hours}) + (20 \text{ employees} \times 40 \text{ hours})]}{1{,}000 \text{ SVH}}$$

The evidence from a larger study conducted by Schuster (1983, 1984a, 1984b) allows limited ability to compare the relative effectiveness of the three separate gainsharing programs. Overall, he concludes that the Scanlon program is the best, and its effects seem to be longer lived than those of the Rucker and Improshare programs. Hammer (1988) argues that these results may be attrib-

Table 2.4 (Continued)

```
                    IMPROSHARE BONUS CALCULATION

Current month:

    Production levels:  Product A = 900 units
                        Product B = 600 units

        Product A = 0.4 WHS x 900 units x 1.8 BPF =       648
        Product B = 1.2 WHS x 600 units x 1.8 BPF =   + 1,296
        Improshare hours                                1,944
        Actual hours (production and nonproduction)   - 1,600
        Hours saved                                       344

    Employee bonus: (the typical employee share is 50 percent)

        Thus, 50 percent x 344 hours saved = 172 bonus hours

           172 bonus hours
        ----------------------- = 10.75%  bonus share
         1,600 actual hours
```

Joe Smith's payroll record for this month might look like this:

Name	Monthly pay	Bonus percent	Bonus	Total pay
Joe Smith	$2,000	10.75%	$215	$2,215.00

Source: Modified by permission from (p. 317) of Productivity Through People by William B. Werther, William Ruch, and Lynne McClure;

uted to the fact that of all three programs, Scanlon requires the most commitment to and institutionalization of worker participation.

NONGAINSHARING PROGRAMS

Some labor-management cooperative programs do not directly tie productivity to employee pay, but they do involve a change in the nonmonetary reward structure as part of their intervention. These nongainsharing programs include quality circles and labor-management committees (See Table 2.5)

Quality Circles

Nongainsharing programs aimed at improving the quality of work life for employees operate under a variety of popular titles: labor-management participation teams, operating teams, quality-

Table 2.5
Comparison of Nongainsharing Programs

Dimension	Quality Circles	Labor-Management Committees
Philosophy	People capable/willing to offer ideas/ make suggestions; improve working environment	Improved attitudes; trust
Primary goal	Cost reduction, quality; improved psychological well-being and job satisfaction	Improve labor-management relations, communications
Subsidiary goals	Attitudes, communication, work behaviors, quality, productivity	Work behaviors, quality, productivity, cost reductions
Worker participation	Screening (1), ad hoc committees and circles (many)	Visitor sub-committees (many)
Suggestion making	Context of committee	None, informal
Role of supervisor and managers	Committee and circle leaders/facilitators	Committee members
Bonus formula	All savings and improvements retained by company	All savings and improvements retained by company
Role of union	Tacit approval	Active membership
Impact on management style	Somewhat	Somewhat

Source: Michael Schuster, Union-Management Cooperation: Structure, Process, and Impact (Kalamazoo, MI: W. E. Upjohn Institute for Employment Research, 1984), pp. 76-77.

of-work-life committees, and quality circles. While there are subtle differences among these nongainsharing options, these differences, according to Cooke (1990), have less to do with structure and purpose, and more to do with the intensity of activity (e.g., the number of employee participants), the emphasis placed on project outcomes (e.g., productivity, absenteeism, communication), the degree of autonomy granted to the group, and the degree of participation by the union. A distinction, therefore, will not be made among these nongainsharing ventures, but rather will be discussed under the generic descriptor *quality circles.*

Quality circles (QCs), are generally defined as "small groups of volunteers from the same work area who meet regularly to identify, analyze, and solve quality and related problems in their area of responsibility" (Munchus, 1983, p. 255). Keys and Miller (1984) note that the historic roots of QCs are imbedded in the human-relations movement represented by such scholars as Argyris, McGregor, and Likert. Related research also suggests that QCs were not devised by the Japanese, as many have assumed, but are an American invention that were first adopted by the Japanese (Cole, 1980). Griffin (1988, pp. 338–339) explains that Japanese "managers have historically been more receptive and committed to employee participation in the workplace than have American managers. Given that QCs are basically formal mechanisms for channeling and directing employee participation, it follows logically that QCs would be more widely adopted in Japan than in the United States."

As the Japanese became more competitive in world markets, however, U.S. managers developed an interest in their styles of management generally and in the concept of QCs in particular. Today, QCs have become the most popular form of labor-management cooperation in the United States, with significant representation in union and nonunion firms (Cascio, 1991). Ingle and Ingle (1983), for example, found that close to 4,000 U.S. firms have implemented QCs. Moreover, Ledford, Lawler, and Mohrman (1988) estimate that in the United States alone, there are currently several hundred thousand QC members. According to Gryna (1981) and Ledford et al. (1988), most QCs use a standard and rather straightforward set of design characteristics, which are presented in Table 2.6. Fossum (1989) and Verma and McKersie (1987) note further that involvement in QCs appears to be most attractive to younger employees, who have had experience with other employee-management participation programs.

Table 2.6
Characteristics of Quality Circles

1. **Objectives**	To improve communication, particularly between line employees and management. To identify and solve problems, including, but not limited to, quality, productivity, cost, safety, morale, housekeeping, and environment.
2. **Voluntarism**	Membership is voluntary among rank and file. Management participation may or may not be voluntary.
3. **Membership**	Individual QCs consist of a leader and 8 to 10 employees from a particular work area.
4. **Meetings**	QCs usually meet once a week, for about one hour, on company time.
5. **Training**	Members receive training in group process and problem-solving techniques.
6. **Rewards**	No monetary awards are given to members. Members receive intrinsic satisfaction from solving problems and observing their implementation.
7. **Information**	QCs typically are not provided with systematic data on company performance, costs, and long-range plans.

QCs and gainsharing programs not only differ in terms of their philosophy toward economic incentives, but also in their number of participants, with QCs having more members per committee. Moreover, unlike the gainsharing programs, the jurisdiction for problem-solving activity for QCs tends to be limited to the unit within which the participants work.

Labor-Management Committees

As Table 2.6 illustrates, while QCs are rather neutral about the role of unions, labor-management committees underscore it. That is, Area-Wide Labor Management Committees (AWLMC) are sponsored by both union and management in a particular geographic area or industry. Fossum (1989, p. 350) notes that the overall mission of AWLMCs is not to engage in collective bargaining activities per se, but rather to "serve as advisory units to deal with employment issues jointly experienced by their constituents."

The administrative structure of an AWLMC consists of an executive director, who is hired jointly by top-level union and management officials in the sector within which they operate; an area-wide advisory committee, with labor and management receiving equal representation; and local labor-management committees, which function at the plant level and, thus, focus on specific problems that face their respective organizations. AWLMCs engage in four primary activities: sponsor social events to improve labor-management relations, provide assistance in negotiations, promote local economic development, and develop and assist plant-level committees (Fossum, 1989; Leone, 1982).

To encourage the formation of AWLMCs, and their plant-level corollaries, the U.S. Congress passed the Labor-Management Cooperation Act in 1978. This piece of legislation amended the Taft-Hartley Act to permit labor-management committees to be funded by employer payments made pursuant to a collective bargaining agreement. Prior to this, U.S. courts had consistently ruled that such fraternization was illegal. Other objectives of the Labor-Management Cooperation Act include the following:

1. to improve communication between representatives of labor and management;
2. to provide workers and employers with opportunities to study and explore new and innovative joint approaches to achieving organizational effectiveness;
3. to assist workers and employers in solving problems of mutual concern not susceptible to resolution within the collective bargaining process;
4. to study and explore ways of eliminating potential problems that reduce the competitiveness and inhibit the economic development of the area or industry;
5. to enhance the involvement of workers in making decisions that affect their working lives;

6. to expand and improve working relationships between workers and managers; and
7. to encourage free collective bargaining by establishing continuing mechanisms for communication between employers and their employees through federal assistance to the formation and operation of labor-management committees.

Of particular interest to AWLMCs is that the Labor-Management Cooperation Act authorizes the federal government to issue grants to labor-management committees, when deemed necessary and appropriate for their implementation or survival. Availability of such funds, however, has recently been radically reduced due to budgetary constraints.

Research on Nongainsharing Programs

Several studies have been conducted to determine the effectiveness of QCs, yet most of them lack the necessary rigor to make them truly informative assessments. In their review of the literature, for example, Steel and Shane (1986) are highly critical of the quality of available research in the area and recommend that conclusions not be drawn until researchers adopt a more scientific approach in their analyses of these programs. They note:

> The majority of studies constituting the quality circle evaluation literature are, at best, flawed and, at worst, potentially misleading. If the level of scientific rigor found in other field research domains such as job redesign, survey feedback, and goal setting may be employed as a yardstick, then the quality circle literature exhibits generally inferior quality (pp. 450–451).

To make matters even more frustrating, recent scientific investigations of QCs provide mixed findings concerning their effectiveness with respect to organizational performance. Marks, Mirvis, Hackett, and Grady (1986), for example, conducted a longitudinal field experiment of a QC in a manufacturing organization. Their results reveal a moderate increase in productivity along with a significant decrease in absenteeism. Furthermore, Havlovic (1991), using monthly longitudinal human-resource-archival data (48 months of pre-QC measure and 81 months of post-QC measures) gathered at a unionized manufacturing firm, attributes a significant reduction in absenteeism, minor accidents, grievances, and quits to the implementation of a QC program.

On the other hand, Mohrman and Novelli (1985) collected data at four-week intervals from one year prior to the implementation of a QC to one year following its implementation in a warehouse operation. They found that QCs had little if any effect on operation efficiency and effectiveness, as measured by costs, throughput costs, labor costs as a percentage of total costs, overtime costs, absenteeism, and accident rates. Likewise, in their study of three U.S. Navy operations, Atwater and Sander (1984) observed no positive effects of QCs on organizational performance, absenteeism, and accident rates.

Research on the attitudinal effects of QCs is somewhat more promising, however. Cooke (1990) surveyed 110 plant managers and 65 local union leaders regarding their attitudes toward employee participation. He found that approximately 60 percent of the respondents perceived a substantial improvement in labor-management relations following the implementation of a quality-of-work-life program. His results also reveal that over 40 percent of the union leaders felt that employee participation enhanced the quality of work life for employees.

Studies of AWLMCs generally, and plant-level labor-management committees in particular, have also been plagued with inferior methodological designs. Indeed, the only comprehensive study in this area was conducted by the U. S. Department of Labor (1990). And while the findings provide unequivocal support for the effectiveness of labor-management committees, the data consisted of mere qualitative appraisals of the accomplishments of these committees in various settings. In commenting on the poorly designed research of AWLMCs, Fossum (1989, p. 551) points out that the effectiveness of labor-management committees is "difficult to assess because in many areas they do not encompass all employers and all employers are not facing the same types of problems." As to the fundamental operations of AWLMCs, Ahern (1982) and Fossum (1989) note that evidence does suggest that they need the support of the major employers and unions within their particular sectors as well as competent executive directors, who are willing to make a long-term commitment to the accomplishment of their goals.

APPROPRIATE STRUCTURE OF JOINT LABOR-MANAGEMENT PROGRAMS

From the review of the literature on gainsharing and non-gainsharing labor-management programs, two major conclusions about the structure of labor-management programs surface, one involving the level of union participation in labor-management programs, and the other dealing with the relationship of the grievance process to these programs. The first conclusion is that labor-management programs seem to function more effectively when the union takes part in them, apparently because the workers perceive their participation as more legitimate with union involvement than without it (Verma & McKersie, 1987). In a related explanation, Kelley and Harrison (1991) suggest that nonunion labor-management programs are less successful because they generally do not offer the workers an opportunity to achieve outcomes that also empower them. Kelley and Harrison assert that with nonunion programs, "the narrow focus and limited objectives for which these programs were designed are quite possibly frustrating these aspirations, undermining the trust and commitment so necessary for success" (p. 46).

Second, the grievance procedure is an important channel of communication that can identify problem areas in the organization (Briggs, 1981; Duane, 1979; Slichter, Healy, & Livernash, 1960).

For this reason, managers of nonunion firms have long recognized the importance of providing employees with feedback mechanisms that facilitate the voicing of worker complaints (Gordon & Miller, 1984). Understandably, therefore, even under a collective bargaining arrangement, where many issues are explicitly excluded from consideration by labor-management programs, many of the problems and complaints raised during the grievance or feedback processes will serve as a catalyst for identifying issues that labor-management programs will address. Moreover, the residual feelings and attitudes about the manner in which the other side has approached grievance resolution in the past are likely to help define the substantive and interpersonal parameters when the parties decide to establish a labor-management program. Thus, it is submitted that a well-functioning grievance procedure is an important precondition for productive labor-management programs. Indeed, Eaton, Gordon, and Keefe (1992) found that worker perceptions of the grievance process tended to be strong determinants of how well QCs functioned.

There are, however, several conditions that moderate the effects of union participation and design of the grievance machinery on program performance. Cotton, Vollrath, Froggatt, Lengnick-Hall, and Jennings, (1988), for example, note that the effectiveness of labor-management programs is contingent on their contextual design, which consists of the level of employee participation, the nature of the decision, and the characteristics of subordinates. Moreover, they recommend that interactions among the various gainsharing and nongainsharing programs should be considered. Indeed, assuming that different types of programs are associated with different outcomes, the combination of a gainsharing program with one that is nongainsharing may prove to be fruitful. To illustrate, an informal QC may be more effective in an organization where other formal participation schemes already exist.

Cooke (1990), Macy and Peterson (1981), and Nurick (1982) also report that workers who participate in joint labor-management activities tend to perceive them more positively than do those workers who do not do so. Moreover, programs that focus on the redesign of subordinates' jobs will have longer-lasting and more positive effects on productivity and workers' attitudes than will those that do not take this approach. Finally, labor-management programs tend to be less effective and eventually die without a commitment to participative management by top-level executives. At minimum, this will entail substantial time and monetary investments in training opportunities to equip individuals with the knowledge, skills, and attitudes necessary for productive participation in these programs (Cascio, 1991).

CONCLUSIONS

This chapter makes it clear that the success of labor-management cooperative programs is contingent on the ability of the participants to sustain high levels of trust. Kochan, Katz and McKersie (1986) argue that the maintenance of trust depends on the amount of support that these programs receive from the upper echelons of the industrial relations systems; for it is there that overall strategies are formulated, modes of interactions are defined, and resource allocations are made.

But this is not a one-way relationship. When plant-level grievances or problems are resolved amicably, or collective bargaining outcomes are achieved through cooperation and trust, acceptance tends to filter up the industrial relations hierarchy. Chamberlain and Kuhn (1986, p. 463) assert that there are numerous examples of labor-management activities "where local unions have quietly disregarded the instructions of national offices and where local plant mangers have violated the limits of their discretion because they recognized that their successful relationships depended on terms differing from those which had been prescribed for them by higher authorities within their respective organizations." And it is this form of interaction that further promotes productive joint programs.

For the research community, this chapter offers substantial exploratory opportunities to the extent that it uncovered several methodological problems concerning past studies of labor-management programs. In what remains of this chapter, some recommendations on how to improve the research methodology for future investigations of labor-management programs are offered. Specifically, studies of these programs should address the following:

1. *Design Characteristics.* The specific characteristics of the program should be identified and described in detail. This is particularly important when attempting to draw conclusions about the relative effectiveness of the various programs.
2. *Age of the Program.* Programs appear to experience an identifiable life cycle, with their effects dependent on where they are located in their individual cycles. Accordingly, an assessment of a program's life cycle should be made.
3. *Assessment of Implementation.* Quality studies of joint programs will delineate the degree to which the union is involved in them, whether top-level management supports them, and whether a consultant was used in either their development or their implementation.
4. *Performance Data.* In measuring the effectiveness of joint programs, researchers by and large have used ill-defined performance measures; therefore, care should be taken to provide clear operational definitions of these constructs. Studies assessing the effects of joint programs on efficiency, for example, should be explicit about the method(s) used for calculating savings and costs (Ledford et al., 1988).
5. *Causality.* The objective of many studies of joint programs is to assess their effects on other labor-management activities. While there are certain techniques, such as path analysis, that are used to attribute causality from data collected at one time, the results of such studies are difficult to interpret and are themselves open to criticism.

Consequently, when attempting to attribute certain effects to joint programs, studies must be based on longitudinal data.

6. *Nonlinear Relationships*. Almost all of the statistical studies in this area assume linearity of relationships, when in fact nonlinear descriptions might be more accurate. Many statistical software packages are available that have the capabilities of examining nonlinear relationships.

Clear and definitive conclusions about the specific effects of labor-management programs cannot be made without well-designed studies of them. It is hoped that these recommendations will encourage such research.

3

Contract Negotiations

As the LMR model indicates (see Figure 1.1), contract negotiations are influenced by the grievance process and subsequently generate outcomes for both parties. The objectives of this chapter are to discuss the recent history of labor-management relations, with particular emphasis on the contract-negotiations process, and to offer some recommendations for promoting cooperative contract negotiations.

RECENT HISTORY OF LABOR-MANAGEMENT RELATIONS

Prior to the 1930s, employment contracts were essentially driven by classical economic theory, where labor was viewed as another economic commodity to be regulated by the marketplace. Accordingly, unions were not particularly attractive to the average worker. The unfolding of the New Deal labor relations system in the mid-1930s, with its supportive collective bargaining legislation and governmental programs, radically changed this attitude. Indeed, early labor leaders, such as Samuel Gompers and Adolph Strasser, would never have anticipated the positive developments that took place in the American labor movement during this period. In point of fact, the proportion of nonagricultural employees represented by unions in the United States grew from 11.2 percent in 1930 to more than 35 percent by 1955. Kochan, Katz, and McKersie (1986, p. 31) add that along "with increasing membership, unions were able to spread into an expanding array of working conditions. Negotiated agreements grew in length and complexity and thereby codified the detailed regulations governing the expanding array of provisions on wages, fringe benefits, and other working conditions."

During the late 1940s and early 1950s, management grew increasingly impatient with the relatively new role that unions played in the workplace. Peterson (1990) and MacDonald (1967) recount that, during this period, several employers tried to short-circuit the collective bargaining process through such initiatives as Boulwarism. With this approach, management sought to take control of the employee-employer relationship by directly polling workers regarding their positions on terms and conditions of employment and, subsequently, fashioning contractual provisions, which were presented to the union as final offers. Even though unions challenged, and eventually persuaded the National Labor Relations Board (NLRB) and the courts, that such practice violated the good-faith provision of the NLRA, management's aggressive bargaining agenda had been established. And during the 1958-59 national recession, efforts to roll back the size of wage settlements and to revoke work rules were met with some success in industries such as electrical products, airlines, and railroads (Mitchell, 1982).

In the 1960s and early 1970s, the civil-rights movement, urban riots, the Vietnam War, along with an overall concern for social issues enhanced public support for collective action, but not for unionism. To explain, the strong economic growth, due in large part to President Kennedy's tax cuts and the Vietnam War buildup, produced tight labor markets, increased worker power, and rank-and-file militancy, aimed not only at management in the form of unofficial wildcat strikes, but at union leadership as well. Kochan (1980, p. 45) contends that "during this time, the rate of rank-and-file rejections of bargaining agreements began to rise. Thus, the rank and file were putting increased pressures on their leaders to revise upward their bargaining goals in response to the tighter labor markets and increases in the cost of living."

Another development that contributed to the deterioration of organized labor's position in American society was the AFL-CIO's support of U. S. participation in the Vietnam War, even after public opinion had shifted against it. Many unions were also quite open in their opposition to civil-rights, environmental, and consumer-protection legislation. These developments led the public to perceive labor as just another special interest group. In fact, such language was used in criticisms of Walter Mondale when he accepted labor's endorsement in the 1980 presidential campaign (Piore, 1991).

Evidence of the labor movement's eroding support came in the form of unsuccessful union organizing campaigns in the private sector, particularly in the new industries, particularly high technology. As a result, union membership declined from 31.4 percent in the early 1960s to 27 percent a decade later. In order to offset this trend, labor organizations turned to the public sector, with significant investments in lobbying activities for labor legislation at all governmental levels. By and large, these activities were responsible for President Kennedy's decision to issue Executive Order 10988, granting federal employees basic bargaining rights, and for the passage of collective bargaining legislation at the state level, which, by the early 1970s, included most of the industrialized states (Burton & Thomason, 1988). Thus, while overall union participation declined during this period, the proportion of membership in public-sector unions grew from 10.6 percent in 1960 to 36.2 percent in 1976.

Although the labor movement experienced some structural and demographic changes during the 1950s, 1960s, and early 1970s, the collective bargaining process remained essentially the same, with management and the unions struggling to negotiate portions of the proverbial fixed pie. By the mid-1970s, however, several forces emerged that significantly affected the traditional bargaining model. That is, private-sector union membership continued to decline, while the union-nonunion wage differentials grew, from 19 percent in the late 1960s to 30 percent by the late 1970s. Deregulation in many industries made it even more difficult for unionized firms to compete with their nonunion counterparts. But, perhaps the most important force was the changing global marketplace. For example, the U.S. import penetration ratio (value of imports over total value of domestic shipments and imports) for all manufacturing increased from 7 percent in 1974 to 13 percent by the mid-1980s. And although U.S. exports rose after 1983, total goods and services imports have continued to outperform exports, "a difference that reached as high as $130 billion in 1986 but narrowed to $56 billion in 1989" (Cooke, 1990, p. 45).

These environmental adjustments not only produced expectations that unions would be willing to make major pay-level and work-rule concessions, but also generated fundamental changes in the bargaining process. Kochan, Katz, and McKersie (1986, p. 128) note:

> These process changes reversed many of the structures, patterns, and procedures that had taken years to build up within bargaining relationships. For that reason, these changes are likely to have longer-lasting effects than many of the pay and work-rule concessions, which may be reversed (less likely for work rules) if and when economic conditions gradually improve and competitive pressures ease.

There is general agreement among scholars and practitioners (Chelius & Dworkin, 1990; Cooke, 1990; Kochan, Katz & McKersie, 1986) that one of the most important changes that occurred was the development of two distinct corporate labor-relations strategies: union avoidance and labor-management cooperation. Each of these initiatives is very different in its approach to the collective bargaining process.

UNION AVOIDANCE

As its name implies, the union-avoidance strategy is highly adversarial, with the ultimate goal of drastically reducing the role of unions in firm operations or by out-and-out getting rid of them. One indicator of the effectiveness of this strategy is the increased number of decertification elections that have occurred over the past few years. In point of fact, the percentage of representation elections that were decertification elections remained almost insignificant (less than 5 percent) prior to 1970. By 1984, however, the number of these elections rose to 875, almost 20 percent of all representation elections that were held that year, with unions winning only 25 percent of them. Carrell and Heavrin (1991) credit the growth of union decertification to aggressive union-avoidance action by a growing number of organized firms.

Union avoiders have been equally strong in their opposition to union-organizing campaigns. Chaison and Rose (1991, p. 26) note:

> Organizing in the United States seems to have drawn the greatest attention [among all other countries with operative labor movements] because it reflects waning union influence and renewed employer assertiveness . . . . The average number of workers won per NLRB election fell from 157 in 1950 to 54 in 1980, while the yield rate, the workers won as a percent of eligible voters, dropped from 84 percent to 34 percent.

In 1991, for a second consecutive year, there was a decline in the percentage of representation elections won by unions. Specifically, labor organizations triumphed in 46.8 percent of the 3,021 elections supervised by the NLRB in 1991, compared with 1990, when unions won 47.6 percent of 3,423 contests.

The union-avoidance strategy has perhaps been most actively pursued in large, "double-breasted" firms (i.e., firms with union and nonunion plants). Managers of these firms have begun to place a high priority on preventing unionization of the nonunion facilities. Data from surveys conducted by Freedman (1979, 1985) reveal that top-level management of 31 percent of double-breasted firms in 1977 and 45 percent in 1983 felt that it was more important for them to keep their nonunion plants union-free than it was to negotiate favorable collective bargaining agreements in their union plants. As Cooke (1990, p. 46) notes, double-breasted union avoiders make "greater capital investments in nonunion plants, reduce employment in unionized plants while increasing employment in nonunion plants, and, where possible seek decertification of unions."

Union avoiders have been particularly resourceful in their approach to contract negotiations. They are, for example, credited with the decentralization of bargaining structures, shifts in the role of industrial relations staff, new communications policies, and a change in the pattern of strike activity (Kochan, Katz & McKersie, 1986). A summary of these tactics is presented in Table 3.1.

Decentralization of Bargaining

At least over economic issues, unions generally favor centralized collective bargaining within an industry or a particular firm. Their intention is to gain the best settlements across contracts or bargaining units by preventing management from whipsawing individual unions against each other. The labor movement, therefore, has long supported pattern bargaining. Kochan (1980, p. 113) defines pattern bargaining as "an informal means for spreading the terms and conditions of employment negotiated in one formal bargaining structure to another. It is an informal substitute for centralized bargaining aimed at taking wages out of competition."

Once an accepted means of negotiations, pattern bargaining has recently been rejected by many union avoiders, who argue that local conditions, among other competitive constraints, precluded the standardization of terms and conditions of employment across bargaining units. Within the trucking industry, for example, the

Table 3.1
Union-Avoidance Strategy: Management's Tactics

Tactic	Description
Decentralization of Bargaining	In an attempt to prevent pattern bargaining, management attempts to focus negotiations on local conditions.
Changing Role of Industrial Relations Staff	Since the training of the industrial relations staff is aimed at perpetuating collective bargaining, their role in negotiations is deemphasized; managers in the financial and operations areas play a more prominent role in negotiations.
New Communications Mode	Management increases its interactions with rank and file, thereby circumventing the traditional management/union communication channels.
Strikebreaking	Management wages an aggressive campaign against strikes, including permanent replacement of strikers.

Source: Concepts abstracted from Thomas Kochan, Harry Katz, and Robert McKersie, The Transformation of American Industrial Relations (New York: Basic Books, Inc., 1986).

impact of the 1982 National Master Freight Agreement declined as regional and company-level modifications and deviations from it surfaced. Furthermore, in 1985, companies that had been covered by the Basic Steel Agreement since 1982 announced that they would bargain separately with the United Steelworkers (USW). Finally, management at Caterpillar, in its recent contract dispute with the United Auto Workers (UAW), refused to engage in pattern bargaining, as the following *Chicago Tribune* report indicates:

> Caterpillar officials have vowed not to accept a contract patterned on other U.S. manufacturers' agreements, notably the pact agreed to last October by Deere & Co. Unlike Deere, Peoria-based Caterpillar exports most of its products and

> needs a "globally competitive" contract, company officials contend.
>
> Likewise, UAW leaders said once more Monday they would never undo the tradition of "pattern" bargaining used by the nation's major industrial unions (Franklin, 1992, p. 14).

At first, both parties held firm to their positions, with the UAW going out on strike and management responding with an employee lockout, coupled with the establishment of procedures for hiring permanent replacement workers. But at this point, management seems to have won the dispute; indeed, the UAW eventually agreed unconditionally to return to work during a cooling-off period, while the parties continue their negotiations. The bottom line here is that the UAW's position at Caterpillar has been substantially weakened by management's outright, and successful, resistance to pattern bargaining. The desperation of those who participated in the strike at Caterpillar is well portrayed in the following comments made by one of them, just hours before he returned to work: "The days of collective bargaining are over. How can unions protect us from management, when they cannot even defend themselves?"

Changing Role of the Industrial Relations Staff

As collective bargaining became a more prominent management responsibility, a need developed for training in the area. Today, almost all undergraduate business administration curricula include courses that cover unions and collective bargaining. Furthermore, many colleges and universities offer graduate and undergraduate labor relations programs, designed to educate the industrial relations professional. The union-avoidance strategy, however, may make this profession obsolete. That is, this strategy prescribes a radical reduction in the control that industrial professionals have over collective bargaining and contract administration. The primary reason for this is that their training is geared toward a working relationship with unions, both at the bargaining table and within the grievance process. Yet, if top-level executives of union-avoider firms want to move away from unionization, such training is not only unnecessary, but is likely to prolong their formal association with unions. Accordingly, in these firms, operations and financial executives, who do not have a professional interest in perpetuating union-management affiliations, have taken a greater role in the labor-relations function. Kochan, Katz, and McKersie (1986, p. 131) comment:

> In order to achieve significant changes in bargaining, the behavior of industrial relations professionals had to change, if this was not possible, the individuals making the key bargaining decisions had to change. In General Motors (GM) these pressures led to a reorganization of the corporate personnel and industrial relations staffs in 1981, as well as the creation of a new strategic-planning group within the industrial relations staff.

New Communications Policies

Another common union-avoidance tactic is to circumvent the union as much as possible, which involves limited communication with union officials. Under the traditional collective bargaining arrangement, management shares information with the union about company performance and ability to pay as well as other pertinent data related to contract negotiations. With this information, the union then packages and passes on to its members only those details deemed appropriate for the union's purpose. The union-avoider communication mode, however, is designed to bypass union officials and to go directly to rank and file with the data that were previously reserved for union officials. To be sure, management is prohibited from negotiating contractual provisions with individual workers; they are not, however, forbidden to provide them with specifics on the firm's financial status and the industry's economic and competitive positions.

American Airlines adopted this method of communication in its 1983 contract negotiations. That is, the company's objectives were to implement a two-tier wage structure and to gain greater flexibility over work rules and personnel deployment. Hence, management felt that while union officials would object to these changes, rank and file might not. As a result, they presented their plans and positions directly to the workers. Kochan, Katz, and McKersie (1986, p. 133) note:

> American began its campaign for new work practices with articles in the company newspaper, home mailings, and video presentations at work. These presentations argued that employment would fall by 50 percent if the carrier's cost structure were not brought down to the level that would make it profitable enough to replace aging aircraft. In return for contract changes, the company offered a series of quid pro quos, lifetime job security for existing workers.

Management also provided rank and file with updates on negotiations, specific union arguments and positions, as well as a "hot line" to answer questions from employees about the process.

The purpose of the union-avoider communication policy is twofold. First, given the highly competitive business climate generated by global and nonunion forces, it gives management an opportunity to build a case for cost-efficient operations, thereby lowering rank-and-file expectations regarding bargaining outcomes. Furthermore, by communicating directly with workers about factors that are intimately tied to the bargaining process, management in a sense has taken a first step toward reestablishing a more direct relationship with individual employees.

Strikebreaking Activities

The final labor-relations tactic used by union avoiders deals with the way they confront strikes. Prior to the 1970s, the strike was an effective economic tool of persuasion. But in the 1980s it became a defensive weapon that unions adopted only as a last resort. The driving force behind this change was an increased willingness by many firms to permanently replace workers on strike. While the NLRA prohibits the permanent replacement of workers on an unfair-labor-practice strike, recent NLRB and court rulings have granted management substantial freedom and flexibility to do so during economic strikes. It is curious that the test case that legitimized this union-avoidance strategy occurred outside of the NLRB's jurisdiction in 1981, when the federal government replaced highly skilled air-traffic controllers, who were engaged in an unlawful strike. Since then, several other firms have broken strikes by permanently replacing their participants, including Phelps Dodge, Florida East Coast Railway, Ravenswood Aluminum, and the *Washington Post*.

Recent attempts by some members of the U.S. Congress to pass a bill making it illegal to hire permanent replacements for those workers on an economic strike failed, and there is little promise of similar efforts succeeding in the near future. As a result, unions have become very sensitive to this union-avoidance tactic; indeed, the mere threat of its implementation has caused them to discontinue their strikes posthaste, as the UAW did at Caterpillar.

Profile of a Union Avoider

Surveys conducted by the Conference Board in 1977 and again in 1980 reveal that the best predictor of future union-avoidance activity is the extent to which a firm's labor force is unionized. Interestingly enough, those firms, whose plants are almost exclusively unionized, are the least likely to adopt a union-avoidance policy. Kochan, Katz, and McKersie (1986) explain that in partially unionized firms, management is generally aggressive in shifting resources to new nonunion facilities, while simultaneously introducing innovative human resource management systems that do not perpetuate the traditional labor-management relationship. Firms that are highly unionized, however, take a much larger risk in implementing such union-avoidance measures. "In these settings, where union avoidance is not a viable short-run alternative for management, we expect to see continued vigorous efforts to innovate at all levels of industrial relations" (Kochan, Katz & McKersie, 1986, p. 239).

Other evidence indicates that firms turn to union-avoidance activity when they experience a rapid increase in import penetration in their primary product markets. It remains relatively unclear why this strategy is preferred over cooperation under these circumstances. Cooke (1990), however, suggests that to remain competitive, these firms must be able to respond quickly to changing environmental conditions, and a collective bargaining arrangement may be perceived by management as incompatible with this needed flexibility.

Labor Movement's Response to Union Avoidance

While management has taken a proactive role in the transformation of U.S. industrial relations, the labor movement has failed to engage in any form of comprehensive strategic planning regarding its future. At best, unions have struggled to develop short-term reactions to management's initiatives. As shown in Table 3.2, these reactions can be characterized by a number of different roles: defender, partner, and cooperator.

Defender. Certain segments of the labor movement have elected to defend their turf by intensifying their attacks on those firms that have embraced the union-avoidance philosophy. Some defenders have engaged in strikes against union avoiders. But ironically, since union avoiders can permanently replace members of an economic strike, management may welcome this response.

A few defenders have combined the strike with a corporate campaign, in which the union embarks on a public relations crusade designed to persuade the firm to change its union-avoidance policies. The first phase of a campaign involves a detailed exploration of a firm's business matters, including any past legal violations as well as the firm's relationship with key suppliers, customers, and financial backers. The second phase consists of

Table 3.2
Union-Avoidance Strategy: Union's Roles

Role	Description
Defender	The union resorts to aggressive tactics, including strikes, corporate campaigns, and in-plant activities, e.g., working-to-rules.
Partner	The union attempts to become associated with management in firm operations by increasing its presence at the upper levels of the decision-making hierarchy, including representation on board of directors and by instituting co-ownership procedures, e.g., Employee Stock Ownership Programs (ESOPs).
Cooperator	The union attempts to develop a cooperative relationship with management. Tactics include joint labor-management programs, cooperative collective bargaining, and cooperative grievance processing.

publishing material detrimental to the firm and in support of the union's demands. At this stage, pressure is also exerted on the firm's key associates to intervene in the dispute.

As a strategy to counteract union avoidance, the corporate campaign has been somewhat successful. For example, it forced J. P. Stevens Company to recognize and collectively bargain with the Amalgamated Clothing and Textile Workers Union. Moreover, when 1,700 unionized steelworkers were permanently replaced at Ravenswood Aluminum Corporation in 1990, the USW decided to wage a rather complicated, global corporate campaign against the company. The focus of this campaign has been on Marc Rich, who controls the company and is a billionaire fugitive whose commodities-trading empire spans 40 countries. Accordingly, the USW enlisted foreign unions to put pressure on Rich. The final straw came when East European unions disrupted Rich's expansion effort in Czechoslovakia, Romania, and Russia. Soon after, the company's chairman was replaced by a Rich associate who agreed to restart contact talks with the union. And on May 26, 1992, the USW received a contract offer from Ravenswood Aluminum Corporation which was later endorsed by the rank and file. What remains is the problem surrounding the reinstatement of the union members, since the company has legal obligations to the workers who permanently replaced the strikers. The early success of the multinational corporate campaign does appear to have given the labor movement a glimmer of hope. Indeed, the UAW, which has been relatively unsuccessful in using only the strike against Caterpillar, is considering a similar campaign, combined with in-plant action, specifically working-to-rules.

Under the working-to-rules policy, employees "refuse to perform activities outside of their job descriptions, follow procedures to the letter, and refuse overtime and other employment duties that might be voluntary" (Fossum, 1989, p. 329). While this tactic generally complies with the contract and company regulations, thus seldom resulting in disciplinary action, its long-term effect is decreased productivity. By lowering productivity, however, a defender only encourages management to outsource, to consider other modes of production, or to develop or bolster its antiunion campaign. As with the economic strike, therefore, the working-to-rules response may actually contribute to the demise of a union.

Partner. To counter union-avoidance activities, some labor organizations have attempted to better position themselves in the business-decision process by obtaining representation on boards of directors, as happened at Chrysler, Pan Am, Eastern Airlines, Western Airlines, and several trucking firms. Similarly, some unions (e.g., those at Chrysler, Eastern Airlines, National Steel Corporation, Rath Packing) have pushed for Employee Stock Ownership Programs (ESOPs), granting workers shares of stock in exchange for labor concessions. For a variety of reasons, attempts to become business partners with management have produced poor to mixed results for the labor movement. First, management has typically been very resistant to the union's participation at this level of business operations. Indeed, unions have only been able to take on the role as partner in highly organized firms, where there has been little application of union-avoidance strategies. Second, government regulations prohibit management and unions from becoming too cozy with each other, which is likely to occur when both of them are involved in high-level strategic planning. Thus, even with the best intentions, the parties are limited in defining the direction of their relationship. Finally, union officials, themselves, have been hesitant in becoming fully immersed in top-level management activities. As Kochan, Katz, and McKersie, (1986, p. 180) note, "some union leaders argue that getting involved with management breaks with revered traditions and threatens to erode the independence that historically gave unions the bargaining power needed to achieve their hard-won collective bargaining gains." In fact, the Teamsters, in their stock ownership agreements with several trucking firms, have been resolute about the extent of control members should have over management decisions, and thus have placed a ceiling of 49 percent on workers' ownership of participating firms.

Defender and partner unions differ in their fundamental philosophies of labor-management relations. The defender union is resigned to the fact that the labor movement as a whole may be in jeopardy and that its particular relationship with management is essentially dispute driven, with gains made only through the exercise of bargaining power. The partner union, on the other hand, sees some promise in working with management, but is not necessarily willing, for whatever reason, to fully pursue cooperative relations. The point here is that the partner role is a distinct strategic choice that may or may not be accompanied by cooperation. Unions that adopt the next role, however, have decided to move in that direction, either as an extension of the partner role or as a strategic choice that is independent of it.

Cooperator. In Chapter 2 it was noted that certain factions of the labor movement have been willing to engage in joint labor-management projects in an effort to convince management that organizational performance can be improved with union assistance. Some unions have even extended this goodwill to the bargaining table, by making concessions on such contractual issues as scheduling changes, frequency of breaks, and management flexibility in making employee work assignments (Holley & Jennings, 1988). Indeed, work-rule concessions were made during the 1982 negotiations over revisions to the National Master Freight Agreement, permitting over-the-road truck drivers, who haul partial loads, to make local pickups.

Some industrial relations scholars have argued that a variation of this form of cooperation is the willingness to establish two-tier wage structures. Under a two-tier compensation system, new hires are paid at lower rates than senior workers, who perform essentially the same jobs. Carrell and Heavrin (1991, p. 178) provide the following examples of two-tier wage structures:

- At Packard Electric, new hires are brought in at 55 percent of the wages of current employees.
- At General Motors' Delco Products plant in Rochester, New York, new assemblers earn up to $9.68/hour, while those with several years' seniority earn up to $13.00/hour.
- Newly hired journeymen at the Ingalls Shipbuilding Company in Pascagoula, Mississippi, earn $1.00 less than the senior employees. The wages of new hires catch up after 2,000 hours.
- Giant Foods negotiated a new entry-level wage of $5.00/hour compared with $6.95/hour in the old contract.
- The Allied Industrial Workers of America union accepted from Briggs & Stratton a pay cut from $8.00/hour to $5.50/hour for new workers on a lower tier.

But many labor organizations have argued that this level of cooperation goes too far, noting that it undermines the principle of *equal pay for equal work.* Indeed, the UAW, which adopted a defender role in its negotiations with Caterpillar, refused to endorse a secondary pay scale in which newly hired employees at the company's parts network would make less than half of that paid to the average assembly-line worker.

Assessments of the effects of two-tier wage systems have been mixed. American Airlines, for example, credits an estimated savings of $100 million in 1984 to its two-tier plan (Duane, 1991a). Similarly, Milkovich and Newman (1990) comment that, at least in the short term, wage savings mount quickly as turnover permits substitution of lower-priced employees for their higher-paid predecessors. There is also evidence, however, that two-tier programs produce resentment, high absenteeism and turnover, and a decrease in productivity (Carrell & Heavrin, 1991). Using efficiency wage models, for example, S. Thomas (1989) reveals that two-tier systems may end up lowering productivity while actually increasing labor costs.

In short, out of a sense for survival, some unions have attempted to initiate cooperation with management, while others have done so simply to make the firm more competitive. Obviously, of the three roles, this one is the most risky. In particular, when a union shares sensitive information about itself with management, which is necessary within a true cooperative mode, the potential for exploitation is tremendously high. To reduce the risk, therefore, a union may want to first experiment by making cooperative gestures to management regarding rather simple, inconsequential matters. If successful, the focus may then move to more substantive issues. And, in fact, there are numerous firms that have responded positively to attempts by unions to build more productive relations. For instance, when it was on the brink of bankruptcy in 1979, Chrysler did not attempt to bust the UAW. On the contrary, the company used UAW concessions to orchestrate a $1 billion loan from the federal government; in return, Chrysler gave the UAW a no-layoff guarantee for an extended period of time. Carrell and Heavrin (1991, p. 208) comment that the "giveback negotiations of the UAW and Chrysler were historic in the labor relations field. . . . The negotiations also proved that a giant corporation and a major union could work together to keep the company operating." In the next section, labor-management cooperation as a corporate strategy is discussed in more detail.

LABOR-MANAGEMENT COOPERATION

Albeit rare, managers at some unionized firms have endorsed a labor-management cooperation strategy. For them, the union is an important member of the family. Indeed, a labor-management relationship is much like a marriage. Within both types of relationships, the parties are bound to each other for an indefinite period of time; they reach an agreement that each participant must live with on a daily basis; they fight periodically, with many attempting to settle their problems among themselves, while others seek to terminate their relationship. To extend this analogy a bit further, just as the divorce rate has increased over the past few years, so has the number of firms seeking a split with their unions. This is not to say, however, that marriage should be avoided or that unions and management are incapable of developing productive associations. What is being said is that labor-management cooperation will require a great deal of effort, commitment, and understanding on the part of both sides.

The first comprehensive treatment of nonadversarial or cooperative collective bargaining was by Walton and McKersie (1965) in their publication *A Behavioral Theory of Labor Negotiations*, and later fine-tuned by Fisher and Ury (1981) in their little book, *Getting to Yes*. A common theme of both books is that the fundamental structure of cooperative collective bargaining consists of a process for identifying common goals and one for achieving them. But labor and management rarely perceive collective bargaining as having cooperative potential; rather they automatically assume that it is an adversarial exercise aimed at dealing with divergent interests. Thus, the key to cooperation is to convert a win-lose relationship into one where both sides can potentially benefit. In the remainder of this section, two major types of incentives for cooperative collective bargaining will be explored: controlling issues and establishing and maintaining integrative frameworks.

Controlling Issues

Several scholars of conflict management (e.g., Fisher & Ury, 1981; Lewicki & Litterer, 1985) advocate strategies of issue control in negotiations as a means of promoting cooperation. The basic premise here is that within the traditional bargaining structure, conflict escalates over bits and pieces of issues until it reaches an unruly mass. Lewicki and Litterer (1985, p. 290) argue that the "problem for negotiators in escalated disputes, therefore, is to develop strategies to contain issue proliferation, and reduce the disputes to manageable proportions."Accordingly, based on the works of Fisher (Fisher, 1964; Fisher & Ury, 1981), they propose some approaches for reducing conflict situations into smaller segments. These approaches include reducing the number of participants on each side, restricting the precedents involved (both procedural and substantive), and depersonalizing bargaining issues.

Reducing the Number of Participants on Each Side. As conflict escalates, each side's inclination is to build its alliances by involving more constituencies in the process. Yet added players tend to exacerbate the conflict, particularly if those who are added have a stake in doing so, as is the case with many professional negotiators. For example, after negotiating several bargaining agreements using the adversarial model, the administrations and unions of three school districts—Livermore Valley and Fairfield-Suisun in California, and Greater Latrobe in Pennsylvania—decided to adopt a more cooperative approach to negotiations. One modification that each of them made was to eliminate the use of professional negotiators, leaving only those people who had a long-term stake in living with the outcomes (Schachter, 1989). In effect, these parties were attempting to control conflict size by returning the issues to the original parties. Lewicki and Litterer (1985, p. 290) note that "the fewer the actors present, or the more the conflict can be limited to two individuals, the more likely the parties will be to reach a favorable settlement."

Restricting the Precedents Involved. A second method for controlling the level of conflict in a bargaining situation is to avoid assuming either procedural or substantive precedents. When the parties enter negotiations with a predetermined notion that they will be conducted as usual, where the objective of each side is to end up with the larger share of the fixed resources, then conflict is certain to escalate. As noted earlier, concession bargaining is an example of how some unions are striving to overcome this tendency. Mills (1989, p. 482) observes:

> According to a survey on concession bargaining, unions have most frequently traded off immediate wage increases or benefits for more employment security. *This is a change from the historic union position* that has been to push relentlessly for job security—guarantees for specific jobs, rather than employment security—guarantees for overall employment levels (emphasis added).

Hirsch (1992) points out that within a good labor relations environment, where both parties adopt forward-looking behavior, bargaining protocols are dispensed with when product and labor markets become unstable. He argues, for example, that for many years the UAW established a bargaining protocol whereby union members received an annual 3 percent increase plus a cost of living allowance (COLA). Under recent General Motors-UAW negotiations, however, the parties agreed to drop this bargaining precedent in light of slow wage growth elsewhere in the private sector, combined with increased foreign competition in the automobile industry. Hirsch concludes that cooperation is contingent on the ability and willingness of the parties to prevent single issues from becoming translated into major questions of precedent.

Depersonalize Bargaining Issues. Perhaps one of the most inflammatory factors in any form of negotiations is when the parties become identified with their positions on issues. By personalizing these positions, the parties get caught up in name-calling, threatening, blaming, point-scoring, among other conflict escalators, thereby diverting their focus on the real issues. Indeed, if a party feels personally attacked, the natural reaction is to grow defensive and to cease listening to the other side's ideas, even when they are worthwhile. Fisher and Ury (1981) suggest that conflict can be contained by restricting discussions to the parties' respective interests. This does not mean that each side must be timid in presenting and making a case for them; in fact,. it would be ill-advised to do so. It does mean, however, that by depersonalizing the negotiations, the parties are more likely to focus on substance, rather than on personal innuendo. Table 3.3 lists some techniques for depersonalizing the collective bargaining process.

Establishing and Maintaining Integrative Frameworks

Another means of converting win-lose situations into mutually satisfying experiences is to establish and maintain integrative frameworks. Lewicki and Litter (1985, p. 295) note that integrative frameworks are ways of defining issues to foster "a common perspective from which initial positions appear more compatible." In what follows, several integrative frameworks are discussed, including establishing commonalities, providing integrative training programs, and promoting cooperative grievance processing.

Establishing Commonalities. One of the most profound barriers to cooperative collective bargaining is the skepticism shared by labor and management regarding any form of interparty collaboration. Chamberlain and Kuhn (1986) point out that although a prima facie case can be made for the preferability of cooperative over adversarial bargaining, both parties have a fundamental fear of union-management cooperation. Accordingly, to engage in genuine cooperative bargaining, they must undergo attitudinal restructuring. One way they can do this is to identify and focus on common issues and objectives. With respect to a unionized firm, for example, labor officials, management, and workers do have different objectives, yet they must work together in some basic

Table 3.3
Techniques for Depersonalizing the Bargaining Process

Technique	Bargaining Statement Examples
Acknowledge the other side's interests	"We understand that the firm must be profitable and productive. After all, it would be terrible for all of us if it could not afford to stay in business." [Union Statement]
Put the problem before your answer	"Last year, the company lost 2 million dollars. We simply cannot afford to repeat such a loss, and I think both sides need to keep this in mind as we negotiate the new contract." [Management Statement]
Be concrete but flexible and innovative	"I know that in the past we have negotiated wage increases on a standard percentage basis, with a COLA provision. We might want to consider a new standard, where wages would be at least partially determined by the level of bargaining-unit productivity." [Union/Management Statement]

Source: Concepts abstracted from Roger Fisher and William Ury, Getting to Yes: Negotiating Agreements Without Giving In (New York: Penguin Books, 1981).

ways or the firm will not remain in operation. Recognition of this mutually shared goal will provide the necessary foundation upon which management and labor can further capitalize on the special contribution each can make to improve organizational performance.

The next step is for the parties to negotiate contractual provisions that recognize common means for improving their firm's performance. While labor-management projects and concession bargaining are well-established instances of this level of cooperation, Chrysler and the UAW have recently experimented with different forms of productivity bargaining. Foremost among their efforts is a far-reaching reorganization of the workplace called a Modern Operating Agreement (MOA). Under the MOA, workers are organized into teams responsible for operations of their departments. This design encourages workers to be more actively involved in quality control as well as more interested in making suggestions for product refinement. Unlike the wage provisions within conventional collective bargaining agreements, MOA wage provisions are based on the number of jobs workers can perform, often referred to as *skill-based pay*. While this new arrangement has not been easy for everyone, both sides agree that for the first time in their long relationship there seems to be a common agreement on how to approach productivity and product-quality issues.

The parties can also establish commonalities through joint efforts to defeat a common enemy. For example, it is not unusual for unions and industry representatives to collaborate in lobbying efforts for special legislation aimed at enhancing the competitive advantage of unionized firms. Chamberlain and Kuhn (1986, p. 454) cite several examples of such action:

> The United Mine Workers and the Bituminous Coal Operators Association have politicked against federal government support for fuels that compete with coal. The Amalgamated Clothing and Textile Workers Union has campaigned for restrictions on textile imports. The Teamsters and trucking associations jointly opposed the deregulation of the trucking industry. The United Automobile Workers show themselves as eager as the automobile company managers to limit Japanese imports.

Providing an Integrative Training Program. Another integrative framework involves providing joint labor-management training. Susskind and Landry (1991) have designed and experimented with a training program whose major objective is to educate union and management in the art of the *mutual-gains approach* to negotiations. Their program consists of the following six steps:

1. *Pretraining private meetings with each side*. The program begins with private meetings between the trainer and leadership on each side. At these meetings, the parties are encouraged to express their concerns regarding the upcoming negotiations (e.g., location of negotiations, agenda of bargaining issues). The trainer then attempts to resolve as many of these concerns as possible. The

objective here is to eliminate those prenegotiation matters that typically generate interparty conflict.

2. *An initial joint training session for labor and management.* Both sides are encouraged to send any and all persons interested to a one-day training session. At this session, the trainer introduces the mutual-gains approach and applies it to conflict situations other than the upcoming contract negotiations, thereby allowing members of labor and management to take a more objective view of the applicability of the mutual-gains approach.

3. *An initial joint training session for members of both bargaining teams.* This session is designed only for those individuals who will be participating in the upcoming contract negotiations. The focus here is on negotiation simulations built around the separate agendas of the parties. At least some of the simulations consist of role reversals. Another "ideal simulation covers internal team bargaining about priorities, the exploration of the other side's interests, opening presentations, the invention of options and packages for mutual gain, and closure on an agreement" (p. 7). This session concludes with debriefing discussions, which are divided into joint reviews of simulation results and into private meetings, where each side can speak freely about their reactions.

4. *A second joint training session for members of both bargaining teams.* At this two-day session, which is held several months prior to the expiration of the current contract, the trainer first reviews the key elements of the mutual gains approach. The participants are then asked to negotiate a written agreement based on their training to date. If the parties are unable to use their newly acquired bargaining skills to reach a mutually satisfying agreement, the trainer shifts into a coaching role in order to facilitate both sides in coming to a joint accord.

5. *Coaching during contract negotiations.* When the parties enter negotiations over the new contract, the trainer should be available as a coach to both sides. It is important to note that the role of the trainer at this point is not to mediate bargaining sessions or to offer solutions to substantive problems in the negotiations,

but simply to assist the parties in executing the mutual-gains process.

6. *Post-contract follow-up aimed at institutionalizing the mutual-gains approach to bargaining and negotiations.* After the parties have negotiated the new contract, the trainer should conduct a debriefing session. The parties should also develop an ongoing quality improvement or joint problem-solving program. In this program, the parties extend the mutual-gains principles to other aspects of their bargaining relationship.

Joint training in the mutual-gains approach is more likely to be effective when both sides are unhappy with the results of previous contract negotiations. In a study of the grievance process, for example, Duane (1984) found several cases where both sides experienced dissatisfaction with their respective bargaining agreements. These parties would be ideal candidates for mutual-gains-bargaining training.

It is also important that the parties' expectations for change not be too unrealistic. In particular, it should be conveyed to them that the training process will require a sustained commitment to a mutual-gains approach to their overall relationship. Thus, it needs to be accompanied by other cooperative support systems: joint labor-management projects and cooperative grievance resolution.

Promoting Cooperative Grievance Processing. The final integrative framework involves promoting cooperative grievance processing. An underlying assumption of the LMR model is that cooperative grievance resolution is a necessary condition for cooperative collective bargaining. Indeed, one would expect the parties to be unable to engage in cooperation over substantive, long-term issues in their relationship, if they are incapable of resolving their day-to-day problems cooperatively. In addressing this concern, Chamberlain and Kuhn (1986, p. 464) make the following observations:

> American labor and management have already gone far toward establishing the basis for a federal system conductive to cooperative bargaining through the grievance process, which

> involves those in shop and office as well as at headquarters in continuous, daily collective bargaining. On the job in the shop or office, workers, managers, and union officials have plenty or opportunity to learn the wisdom of respecting one another's interests and to learn to appreciate the mutual benefits to be gained by bargaining cooperatively. Here, where supervisors, workers, and shop stewards must confront each other daily and join together to produce effectively and efficiently, an appreciation of quid pro quo bargaining is strong. From long practical experience, they have learned to base their cooperation on a realistic appreciation of each other's desire to protect their own interests. And there is available to them the device of the grievance process, through which they may openly discuss their demands, protect their interests, and arrange mutually satisfactory settlements.

As with cooperation in contact negotiations, cooperative grievance processing is an unconventional form of labor-management interaction. Management and labor, therefore, must be convinced that by restructuring their relationship, they stand to benefit more than from retaining their old ways of resolving grievances. To do so, however, may be a formidable job, especially in the case of union avoiders, who have already made a decision that their interests are best served without the union. Therefore, any efforts to make the grievance process a more cooperative experience must take into account the potential benefits of labor-management cooperation, which were discussed in Chapter 1 and will be further addressed in Chapter 4; must be comprehensive and emphasize skill development, involving those activities discussed in Chapters 2 and 3; and must be accompanied by a fundamental understanding of the antecedents to cooperative grievance processing, which will be discussed in Chapters 5 and 6.

CONCLUSIONS

The nature of collective bargaining in the United States is undergoing a substantive transformation. Much of this change has been spearheaded by management in response to increased competition from foreign and nonunion firms as well as to a general erosion of the U.S. economic system. What has emerged are two diametrically opposing approaches to the collective bargaining process: union avoidance and labor-management cooperation. Tactics of the union avoider include decentralization of the bargaining structure, changes in the role of industrial relations staff, new methods of communication with unionized employees, and effective countermeasures to the strike. The labor movement's response to the union avoider has been relatively weak, as illustrated by the decline in the proportion of union membership, the decline in the success of union-organizing campaigns, and the increased number of union decertification elections.

While the union-avoidance strategy has been somewhat effective in limiting the role of unions in the workplace, its long-term effects have yet to be observed. Will it result in increased productivity and product quality, thereby enhancing a firm's competitiveness as its proponents promise? Or will it be associated with precisely the opposite effect? Indeed, those scholars and practitioners who endorse labor-management cooperation comment:

> New quantitative studies indicate that productivity is generally higher in unionized establishments than in otherwise comparable establishments that are nonunion, but that the relationship is far from immutable and has notable exceptions. Higher productivity appears to run hand in hand with good industrial relations and to be spurred by competition in the product market, while lower productivity under unionism appears to exist under the opposite circumstances (Freeman & Medoff, 1984, p. 180).

In other words, when labor and management cooperate, unionized firms are likely to outperform their nonunionized competitors. Labor-management cooperation, therefore, could ultimately provide firms with a distinct competitive advantage.

4

The Grievance Process

A central theme of this book is that the grievance process directly affects such labor-management outcomes as productivity and product quality, while indirectly influencing them through its effects on the parties' interactions at the bargaining table and on joint projects. In this chapter, several key elements of the grievance process are explored: (1) the standard grievance procedure, (2) variations in grievance procedures, (3) the grievance process and firm performance, (4) the grievance process and joint labor-management programs, (5) the grievance process and contract negotiations, and (6) interpreting grievance data.

THE STANDARD GRIEVANCE PROCEDURE

In the early days of collective bargaining, labor and management did not draw a clear distinction between negotiating the agreement and its interpretation and administration. But as contracts became more sophisticated and collective bargaining a more integral part of defining terms of employment, the grievance process gradually became more detached from contract negotiations. During World War II, this policy was further advanced by the War Labor Board, which recommended that all bargaining agreements include separate provisions for multistep grievance procedures, culminating in third-party arbitration. This recommendation received widespread support from the collective bargaining community. Ichniowski and Lewin (1987, p. 164) observe, for example, that by "1944, arbitration provisions were common in some industries, such as steel refining, textiles, petroleum, and aircraft, where over 80 percent of all collective bargaining agreements contained such provisions." Today, as measured by the time, effort, and personnel involved, grievance resolution is the parties' most important activity (Chamberlain & Kuhn, 1986; Thomson & Murray, 1976).

As noted earlier, a grievance can be anything that the parties want it to be, provided that it complies with the appropriate legalities. In general, however, a grievance is a *written* allegation by employees that management has in some way violated their contractual rights (Duane, 1991b). The overall role of the grievance procedure, therefore, is to process such allegations through a succession of steps from lower to higher. Chamberlain and Kuhn (1986) note further that the grievance procedure serves three related functions: (1) it allows the parties to settle differences of opinion about the meaning and interpretation of contractual terms; (2) it provides them with a procedure for addressing new and unforseen circumstances; and (3) it permits adjudication of disputes over the application of general contractual provisions to local conditions.

Roughly 99 percent of all labor-management contracts contain grievance procedures (Holley & Jennings, 1988). While these procedures are as varied as the contracts within which they are found, Table 4.1 presents a fairly representative one.

First Step

The first step of the typical grievance procedure consists of two phases. First, the affected employee, with or without the union steward, discusses the problem with the first-line supervisor. At this phase, the goal should be to resolve the problem as soon and

Table 4.1
Representative Grievance Procedure

Step	Personnel Involved	Action
First Step	Employee (with or without union steward) and first-line supervisor.	Complaint is first discussed; if not resolved, it is reduced to writing and answered by management within 5 days; management's decision may be appealed to the second step.
Second Step	Addition of union grievance committee member and industrial relations representative.	Participants meet to discuss the grievance; management's decision is reduced to writing within 5 days of the meeting; the decision may be appealed to the third step.
Third Step	Addition of top-level union official and industrial relations manager and/or general plant official.	Participants meet to discuss the grievance; management's decision is reduced to writing within 10 days of the meeting; the decision may be appealed to the fourth step.
Fourth Step	Addition of a neutral third party, typically an arbitrator or arbitration panel.	Participants meet to discuss the grievance; within 14 days of the meeting the third-party issues a final and binding decision.

as informally as possible. But if agreement is not reached, the complaint is reduced to writing, thereby technically becoming a grievance, and submitted to management. Within certain time constraints, management issues a decision, which may be appealed by the union steward or the grievant to the second step.

Second Step

At the second step, the grievance is presented to an industrial relations representative by the steward and/or a member of the grievance committee, which usually consists of the local union president or designee, the business agent, the chief steward, and a couple of elected members. The participants at this stage are very familiar with the contract and with grievance precedent. Decisions on second-step grievances are rendered in writing by the industrial relations representative, and appeals must be made within tight time limits, typically five days.

Third Step

Grievances that are appealed to the third step are likely to involve issues that have either precedent-setting ramifications, major cost implications, or broad application within the firm's operation. Due to the importance of these grievances, additional management and union personnel are added to the deliberations, including the industrial relations manager and other management officials, such as a general foreman or plant superintendent, along with top-level union officials.

Holley and Jennings (1988) suggest that this stage of the grievance process serves purposes other than simply resolving the case at hand. First, third-step meetings provide new union officials with a means of on-the-job training. Second, when upper-level management and local union officials get involved, they serve as buck-passing devices for the union steward in the event that the grievance is not resolved in favor of the grievant. Third, this step serves as a therapeutic mechanism for the grievant, who may simply wish to express discontent to upper levels of management. Duane (1979) notes that the third step of the grievance procedure can function as a device that not only detects problems that are common among subunits, but identifies individual subunits that require special attention. To do so, he recommends that third-step grievance rates be thoroughly analyzed.

Fourth Step: Arbitration

If a grievance is not resolved by the third step, it can be submitted to a neutral third party (arbitrator), who hears evidence from both sides and makes a decision which is final and binding on the parties. According to Fossum (1989, p. 376), there are a number of methods for selecting an arbitrator:

> First, the parties may designate the name of a permanent arbitrator in their contract. Second, the parties may petition a private agency, such as the American Arbitration Association, for an arbitration panel. A panel consists of an odd number of members (usually five) from which each party rejects arbitrators in turn until one remains. He or she becomes the arbitrator unless one party objects, in which case a new panel is submitted. Third, the same process may be followed by petitioning the Federal Mediation and Conciliation Service (FMCS), which also supplies panels of arbitrators listed by this agency.

The arbitrator's decision is a written document submitted to the appropriate management and union officials. Its elements usually consist of the following:

1. A statement of the issue(s).
2. A statement of the facts surrounding the grievance.
3. Identification of management and union representatives involved in the case.
4. Relevant bargaining agreement provisions.
5. Summaries of the union and management positions.
6. Discussion and justification for the decision.
7. The award.

An arbitrator's decision need not favor a particular party. Indeed, compromise awards are often delivered. What is important, however, is that the arbitrator must demonstrate a thorough understanding of all the facts and contentions raised in the hearing (Holly & Jennings, 1988).

VARIATIONS IN GRIEVANCE PROCEDURES

While Table 4.1 presents a representative procedure, there are important differences in procedures among certain labor and industrial sectors. For example, special accommodations are generally made for agriculture, construction, and trucking workers. Moreover, procedures in the public and nonunion sectors vary from the standard grievance procedure. Finally, procedures outside of the U.S. industrial relations system have unique features.

Agriculture, Construction, and Trucking Procedures

The design of grievance procedures in contracts covering farm workers differ considerably from the typical procedure. The United Farm Workers (UFW) union, for example, does not have locals and thus lacks the stability of leadership to process grievances that are characteristically subject to the first step. Chamberlain and Kuhn (1986, p. 149) note that members of the UFW

> migrate from one ranch to another as the seasons and harvests change; when a rancher hires a work force at harvest time, union members elect at least one ranch committee that performs many of the functions for which local union officers and shop stewards are responsible in work places of more stable employment. The seasonality of work and the continual turnover among those elected to the ranch committees creates considerable inefficiency in the administration of the agreement and often frustrates quick settlement of grievances.

The construction and trucking industries share many of these same workplace instabilities. In addition, construction foremen are themselves usually union members. As a result, standard grievance procedures do not meet the needs of either the workers or the employers in these industries. Consequently, they have turned to one-or two-step procedures, with the ultimate goal being instant justice. Describing grievance resolution in construction, for example, Mills (1980, p. 88-89) asserts that "when the job steward and the employer's superintendent fail to settle a grievance, the business agent of the local union intervenes. If he is also unsuccessful, a strike is likely to be called on the spot. The grievance, and the strike, are then settled in some manner."

In trucking, the Teamsters have long supported informal and open-ended procedures, with no arbitration, except in the case of discharge. The flexibility of this structure affords little explanation of grievance settlements and discourages precedents, thereby granting union officials a high degree of latitude in presenting their cases. But as Chamberlain and Kuhn (1986) and Levinson (1980) argue, such informality and lack of adherence to legalisms promote favoritism and discrimination among workers.

Public-Sector Procedures

One of the most important differences between public- and private-sector collective bargaining is how the parties resolve their disputes. The channels of appeal in the public sector are somewhat more confusing, since negotiated grievance procedures often compete with established civil-service complaint systems. In the past, some union leaders exploited this confusion by choosing selectively between the two procedures on the basis of which one would be more efficacious for a particular issue. Consequently, some efforts have been made to clarify the process. Executive Order 11616, for example, specifies that federal employees must use civil-service appeal mechanisms to challenge discharges. Even in the case of discharge, however, these employees are granted the right to union representation if desired (Chamberlain & Kuhn, 1986).

The confusion caused by the dual appeal mechanisms in the public sector will not be eliminated until the laws have undergone substantive change. Some informed observers have proposed a comprehensive federal statute dealing with labor relations in the federal, state, and local governments. This change would amend the NLRA to include in its definition of *employer*, federal, state, and local governments. One problem with this proposal is whether or not such legislation would be constitutional. In 1976, for example, the U.S. Supreme Court held unconstitutional the 1974 amendments to the Fair Labor Standards Act, which extended many of its provisions to almost all state employees *(National League of Cities v. Usery*, 1946). In essence, *National League of Cities* made it illegal for the federal government to regulate employment practices of state and local workers. But in 1985 the Court overturned *National League of Cities* and rejected "as unsound in principle and unworkable in practice, a rule of state immunity from federal regulation that turns on a judicial appraisal of whether a particular governmental function is 'integral' or 'traditional' "*(Garcia v. San Antonio Metropolitan Transit Authority*, 1985). Thus, a federal law regulating the collective bargaining activities of public-sector workers, including their rights to a single appeal mechanism, is more likely to withstand constitutional challenges, but "the political prospects for such a law are not promising" (Burton & Thomason, 1988, p. 48).

An alternative to a comprehensive federal statute would be legislation that establishes minimum standards that public-sector employers would have to meet. This law would grant public employees the right to bargain collectively, with limited rights to strike. It would also establish the National Public Employment Relations Commission, which would administer the law (Aaron, 1988). But, most importantly, it would require labor and management to establish a single, orderly impasse procedure for the settlement of their disputes, including grievances.

Nonunion Procedures

Many nonunion companies recognize the benefits of sponsoring feedback mechanisms that facilitate the voicing of complaints and concerns by workers. The structure of these mechanisms varies widely, however. Perhaps the most common nonunion procedure is the *open door policy*. While this mechanism emphasizes resolution of problems as close to the relevant work area as possible, it provides employees with an opportunity to carry their concerns to top-level management, in most cases to the chief executive officer or designee. Diaz, Minton, and Saunders (1987) submit the following variations of the open door policy.

Executive detective: A top-level executive investigates major concerns submitted by employees and recommends appropriate action.
Ombudsman: This is a full-time position held by an executive who assists the parties in negotiating settlements to their disputes.
Management hearing committee: This appeal mechanism is modeled after the union grievance procedure, where a management committee serves as the final step in the progressive review process.

Although rare, some nonunion procedures provide for the final resolution of certain grievances, typically those involving dismissal, by an outside arbitrator, who is selected by the firm and the employee, with the firm paying most of the expenses (Coulson, 1978). Diaz et al. (1987, p. 25) suggest that the neutral third party is added to achieve three objectives: "(1) a complete say for each side in airing the grievance; (2) a strong connotation of justice, since a professional, neutral third party renders decisions; and (3) benefits for both parties based on the opinion of a 'cool-headed' professional."

Other innovative nonunion procedures include the *deep-sensing approach*, which consists of periodic meetings between top managers and groups of employees to discuss current problems or gripes. The Rocketdyne Division of Rockwell International has experimented with a similar approach, called *vertical staff meetings*. Here, a few employees from various organizational subunits are picked at random to meet with the division's president. At these meetings, problems are disclosed and eventually investigated by

Table 4.2
European Grievance Procedures

Country	Procedure
France	Union representatives act only as observers of the process, where a committee of workers, elected by the workers, negotiates grievances with management. French law also requires that grievance procedures include three steps: the presentation of a case first to the supervisor, then to a plant committee, and finally to a labor court. But the worker has the right to go directly to court if he or she desires.
Germany	Grievances are processed through works councils, which are mandated by federal law for all private enterprises with more than five employees, and a system of labor courts: 113 local courts, one court for each state, and one federal appeals court. A grievance can be submitted either by an individual or by collective groups. The courts first try conciliation, which succeeds in roughly one-third of the cases. If conciliation fails, the courts then issue binding decisions.
Italy	Grievance procedures normally have three steps: the factory council, the union and employers' association, and the local court. Italy has no special labor courts; instead, regular local tribunals or magistrates are utilized.
Great Britain	In keeping with its more decentralized bargaining structure, special grievance procedures have been adopted by industry

management (Fossum, 1989). For the workers, this type of procedure gives them a mechanism for articulating their concerns. From management's perspective, it is a means of assessing employee morale, but it also serves as a unique source of information about firm operations.

International Procedures

While the grievance procedure is an issue subject to collective bargaining in the United States, many other countries treat it differently. In Western Europe, for example, the procedures for handling grievances are generally determined by legislative mandate. Moreover, Sauer and Voelker (1993, p. 516) note:

Table 4.2 (Continued)

Country	Procedure
	agreements. Although there is much variation, most are similar to the typical American system, with a series of steps progressing through local, regional, and national levels. There is a notable exception, however. Arbitration as the final step is rarely utilized. Thus, grievance procedures generally end in a final proposal, which the union may accept or reject by striking.
Sweden	Until 1976, management possessed the right to interpret all of the terms in a labor contract, while unions had the right of appeal. In 1976, however, the Act of Codetermination at Work was passed, granting unions the prior right of interpretation over three major issues, including (a) codetermination provisions, (b) provisions regarding disciplinary measures, and (c) a worker's duty to perform certain tasks, with management having the right of appeal over these issues. Swedish law requires that grievances, either labor or management, must be submitted to a three-step procedure: (a) negotiation at the company level, (b) negotiation at the industry level, (c) appeal to the labor court, or to an arbitrator. The parties are forbidden to engage in strikes or lockouts to settle grievances.

Source: Constructed from Thomas Kennedy, European Labor Relations (Lexington, MA: Lexington Books, 1980), pp. 10, 50-51, 95, 179-180; and Robert Sauer and Keith Voelker, Labor Relations: Structure and Process (2nd ed.). (New York: Macmillian, 1993), p. 517.

> The legal nature of worker representation and worker grievance-handling in most European countries, the final settlement of worker-management rights disputes, is usually accomplished in a labor court system. Labor courts are empowered to settle disputes arising not only from collective agreements but also from the application of labor laws or government decrees.

Examples of grievance processing in assorted European countries are presented in Table 4.2.

The European Community (EC) has embarked on a momentous project to unify its 12-member countries. A central objective of this project is the elimination of trade barriers so that people, capital, and goods can move freely within the community. So far, the EC has not specifically addressed grievance-handling mechanisms, but the various labor-relations activities, including collective bargaining and grievance resolution, will be the focus of much debate and controversy in the years ahead.

The relationship between labor and management in Japan is noted for its informal, consultative approach to resolving disputes. As a result, although some enterprise-level collective bargaining agreements contain grievance and arbitration procedures, they are seldom used (Katz & Kochan, 1992). The underlying Japanese philosophy of labor-management relations is that managers and workers are members of a family, where disputes are talked out until a mutually satisfying settlement can be reached. Thus, "the adversarial, legalistic model found in the West is generally unacceptable in Japan" (Sauer & Voelker, 1993, p. 523).

THE GRIEVANCE PROCESS AND FIRM PERFORMANCE

It is well known that grievance procedures are costly to operate. In 1970, for example, General Motors complained that in the previous year "it had paid in its plants more than 13 million dollars to union committeemen who do not work on assembly lines or at machines, but who represent union members in disputes with management" (Serrin, 1973, p. 156). Moreover, when the parties are unable to resolve grievances internally, the union may elect to submit them to arbitration, which can easily exceed $5,000 per grievance (Duane, 1991b). Grievance processing is also time consuming. Dalton and Todor (1981) estimate that, on average, it takes 9.1 workhours to settle a grievance, and this accounts only for the time spent in formal meetings, not preparation time or time devoted to informal deliberations. Finally, grievance procedures limit the flexibility of a firm to terminate unproductive workers and to impose efficient work rules. Not so obvious perhaps are some of the benefits of grievance procedures. To be sure, as noted earlier, they serve as formal systems of communication between management and workers. But the question remains, do such procedures enhance the actual performance of the firm? In what follows, the relationship between grievance procedures and firm performance, as measured by employee turnover, strike activity, and productivity, is examined.

Employee Turnover

Almost all of the research on the relationship between turnover rates and grievance procedures does not directly compare the rates of unionized firms that have grievance procedures with those of nonunionized firms that do or do not have them. Instead, comparisons are drawn between turnover rates of union and nonunion firms, with the assumption that only unionized firms have grievance procedures. The results from this approach consistently suggest that turnover, whether voluntary or involuntary, is lower among unionized firms, after controlling for the wage effect and other relevant factors (Ichniowski & Lewin, 1987). While one might naturally attribute this effect to the existence of grievance procedures in the union sector, this explanation may not be totally accurate. Freeman and Medoff (1984) submit, for example, that what is being observed may not be an absolute grievance-procedure effect, but rather the impact of grievance-procedure type, with nonunion procedures providing employees with a less-effective voicing device. They recommend, therefore, that more sophisticated investigations of the effects of grievance procedures on turnover be conducted.

D. I. Rees (1991) attempted to test the Freeman-Medoff voice model of unionism, using data on New York public school teachers for the period 1975 through 1978. In particular, he explored the relationship between exit behavior and strength of the grievance procedure, as defined by the breadth of conditions that were subject to the grievance process and whether binding arbitration was included. His results indicate that teachers with the two strongest procedures had, on average, a significantly lower probability of quitting than did those teachers working under other types of procedures.This study, however, does not provide a true test of the

Freeman-Medoff voice model, since its sample included only unionized teachers.

Unfortunately, there is no comprehensive study that investigates the effects of union and nonunion procedures on turnover. Yet a series of analyses by Spencer provides important insight into this issue. In the first analysis (Spencer, 1986), he showed that whether or not a union is present, high instances of employee voice mechanisms (e.g., grievance procedures, suggestion systems, employee-management meetings) are associated with lower turnover. A later analysis of these data by Spencer is discussed by Ichniowski and Lewin (1987). In this study, an attempt is made to directly compare the effects of grievance procedures on turnover in unionized firms with those in a nonunion settings. To do so, the following equation is proposed:

$$\text{TURNOVER} = A + \beta_1\text{UGRV} + \beta_2\text{NUGRV} + \beta_3 X + \varepsilon$$

where TURNOVER = the ratio of the number of employees who quit to total number of employees; UGRV = a dummy variable for unionized workers, all of whom have grievance procedures; NUGRV = a dummy variable for nonunionized workers, all of whom have grievance procedures; and X = a set of controls that could influence turnover. The third group of workers in the sample consisted of nonunion workers who do not have access to grievance procedures.

When the equation is estimated, the findings suggest that turnover rates are lower in union and nonunion firms that have grievance procedures than they are in nonunion firms that do not have them. Moreover, when the equation is reestimated, with the nonunion-with-grievance-procedure category divided into two subgroups—those procedures with arbitration and those without it—the results suggest that nonunion firms that have grievance procedures, with or without third-party intervention, experience lower turnover than do those nonunion firms without grievance procedures. Ichniowski and Lewin (1987, p. 179) conclude that "nonunion establishments can implement grievance procedures that effectively lower employee quit rates, and also that a provision for arbitration by an outside neutral is not necessary to achieve lower turnover rates." While these results are noteworthy, a more definitive analysis would have involved longitudinal data (i.e., analysis of turnover before and after grievance procedures were installed) as well as more extensive experimental control.

In short, there is evidence that access to *union-type* grievance procedures, without or with arbitration, tends to reduce quit rates, but is this necessarily good for overall firm performance? Certainly there are costs involved in employee turnover, including separation replacement and training costs. There are, however, costs associated with retaining certain groups of employees (e.g., poor performers or workers with high absence rates). To the extent that grievance procedures protect these individuals, they may actually impede efficiency and effectiveness of firm operations. This issue warrants further attention from researchers. Still, evidence in this section leads to the following proposition:

Proposition 1: Employee access to *union-type* grievance procedures reduces turnover.

Strike Activity

One of the original purposes of the grievance procedure was to reduce the likelihood of strikes. Reynolds et al. (1986, p. 545) note that "a properly constructed grievance procedure capped by arbitration should in principle render work stoppages unnecessary during the life of the agreement." Indeed, there is some indirect evidence that supports this position. In the manufacturing sector, for example, wildcat strikes were common during the 1930s and 1940s, but became less so by the 1950s and 1960s due in part to the spread of grievance procedures. Today, wildcat strikes have become the least important labor-relations activity (Ichniowski and Lewin, 1987).

Unfortunately, while the above indirect evidence exists, there are no systematic studies that compare strike activities of employees who have access to grievance procedures with those who do not. What is available is a study by Brett and Goldberg (1979) of the coal-mining industry, where the rate of wildcat strikes historically has been high. Their results indicate that such strikes were more frequent in mines where workers perceived their supervisors as being incapable of handling grievances or where they could not be resolved locally. Moreover, they suggest that the more robust the procedure the lower the probability of wildcat strikes. Thus,

> Proposition 2: Employee access to *union-type* grievance procedures reduces wildcat strikes.

Productivity

There are several studies that examine the effects of unionism on productivity (for reviews of this literature, see Freeman & Medoff, 1984; Ichniowski & Lewin, 1987). Overall, these studies suggest that unionized firms are generally more productive than comparable nonunion ones. One might expect, therefore, a linear positive association between grievance rates and productivity. But the bulk of the research in this area does not support such a relationship. In fact, several studies suggest that there is a linear negative relationship between grievance rates and productivity (Ichniowski 1986; Katz et al., 1983; Katz, Kochan & Weber, 1985; and Norsworthy & Zabala, 1985).

It could be argued that this negative relationship is industry specific, since three of the four studies analyzed data that were collected from automobile manufacturing firms. Another interpretation is that "a 'displacement effect' is involved; that is, when more time is devoted to grievance handing, less time is devoted to production tasks" (Ichniowski and Lewin, 1987, p. 186). But as Ichniowski (1986) notes, the magnitude of productivity lost in each of the studies is simply too large for this to be the sole reason. A more likely explanation is that the effect is equity based. Indeed, when unionized workers feel they are not being fairly treated by

Figure 4.1
Grievance Rate and Productivity

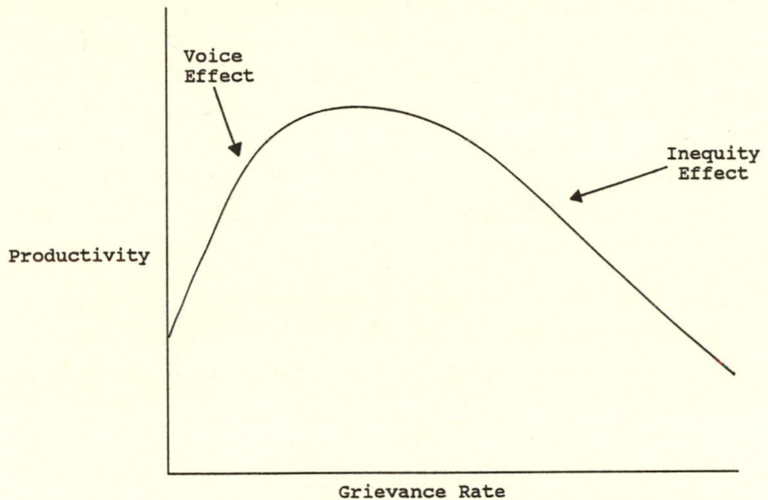

management, they are likely to file grievances. When repeated grievance action fails to rectify the alleged injustice, equity theory (Adams, 1963) predicts that the grievant will turn to other equity-achieving devices, including effort reduction. Thus, contrary to Slichter et al. (1960), who suggest that high grievance rates may signal an open and perhaps a more effective grievance procedure, they may actually indicate that workers and management have difficulty in resolving conflict.

Linear explanations of the relationship between grievance activity and productivity may not tell the whole story, however. It has been maintained throughout this work that the grievance procedure provides employees with a means of communicating with management; therefore, one would expect a positive relationship between grievance action and productivity, at least initially (i.e., voice effect). But as perceived contract violations continue and grievance rates rise along with the intensity of feelings of inequity, reduced work effort will follow, thereby lowering productivity (i.e., inequity effect). This relationship is illustrated in Figure 4.1.

Obviously, the worker-reaction effects will vary depending on the types of grievances filed and the process by which settlements are reached. Still, a zero grievance level does not appear to be optimal for firm performance. This is consistent with the findings of Kleiner, Nickelsburg, and Pilarski (1991), who report that grievance rates have a nonlinear effect on productivity. More important, it helps to explain why unionized plants, which generally have formal grievance procedures, are more productive than nonunion plants. Ichniowski (1986, p. 86) adds:

> Having a grievance procedure can therefore be viewed as a way to reduce the number and duration of worker reaction effects [inequity effects]. More precisely, the presence of a formal grievance procedure will be associated with improved productivity if the procedure reduces the magnitude (number and duration) of worker reaction effects by more than the number of employee hours required to process grievances.

According to Kleiner, Nickelsburg, and Pilarski (1988) the real issue is not how variations in grievance rates influence productivity, but rather how variations in these rates affect profitability. They note that much of the research thus far assumes that "reducing grievance activity increases firm productivity, to the extent that zero grievances might be the amount that would maximize profits" (p. 179). Acknowledging that one of the greatest incentives for grievance action is an increase in production rates, they conclude that the economic gains of the production growth may outweigh those costs related to a rise in grievance activity. At any rate, the LMR model supports the following propositions:

Proposition 3: Employee access to *union-type* grievance procedures increases productivity.

Proposition 4: Grievance rates are nonlinearly related to productivity.

THE GRIEVANCE PROCESS AND JOINT LABOR-MANAGEMENT PROGRAMS

While the underlying assumption of the LMR model is that cooperative grievance resolution contributes to the effectiveness of labor-management projects, little research has been conducted on the relationship between the grievance process and project performance. What is available is a study of the impact of quality of work life programs and grievance system effectiveness on union commitment (Eaton et al., 1992). The researchers conclude that union loyalty is enhanced by an effective grievance procedure, as measured by the workers' perceptions of it. They note further that perceived grievance effectiveness is positively associated with a low perceived threat of joint projects to the union. It seems that such projects "pose a greater threat in situations where the grievance procedure is ineffective and, therefore, unable to promote a sense of justice in the workplace. A corollary of this finding may be that a well-functioning grievance procedure is a *precondition* for member acceptance of QWL [Quality of Work Life programs]" (p. 601, emphasis added). Their results "underscore an important respect in which unions' destinies may be in their own hands; the greater the ability of the union to exercise its traditional role in contract administration, the less concerned are its members about the possible debilitating effects of cooperative activity" (p. 603). As such, the LMR model proposes:

> Proposition 5: Employee access to *union-type* grievance procedures is a precondition for effective labor-management programs.

THE GRIEVANCE PROCESS AND CONTRACT NEGOTIATIONS

Definitive research on the effects of grievance activity on contract negotiations is surprisingly sparse. Indeed, Labig and Greer (1988, p. 19) observe that the "relationship between grievance activity and contract negotiations is not illuminated by past research." Yet, Gandz and Whitehead (1981) and Peterson and Lewin (1981) offer some hypotheses regarding this relationship. In short, they postulate that the manner in which the parties resolve their grievances affects their overall bargaining relationship, including contract negotiations. In other words, cooperative (hostile) grievance resolution promotes cooperative (hostile) contract negotiations. Moreover, Sloane and Whitney (1981) note that the number of grievances is likely to increase as the time for negotiating a new contract approaches, arguing that union leadership drums up grievances to serve special political ends at the bargaining table. This discussion is summarized in the following propositions:

Proposition 6: Cooperative (hostile) grievance resolution promotes cooperative (hostile) contract negotiations.

Proposition 7: Grievance rates increase just prior to contract negotiations.

INTERPRETING GRIEVANCE DATA

A formidable barrier in gaining a better understanding of grievance procedures is the lack of consensus regarding what grievance rates mean and the level at which grievances should be resolved.

Grievance Rates

When describing grievance activity, it is customary to use the grievance rate (i.e., the number of grievances filed per 100 employees per year [Ash, 1970; Begin, 1971; Peach & Livernash, 1974]). But there is no agreement on what constitutes an acceptable rate, with Briggs (1981) recommending a rate below 10, while Begin (1971), McKersie (1964), and Slichter et al. (1960) advocate rates as high as 20. This debate may signify the inappropriateness of assigning a single rate to all labor-management relationships.

Indeed, one would anticipate variations in rates due to such factors as economic and financial conditions, industry effect, and complexity of organizational structure.

Of equal concern is the fact that grievance rates are often used to characterize the temperament of the parties' relationship. Conventional wisdom dictates that high rates operationally define poor relations. But some researchers (Peach & Livernash, 1974; Slichter et al., 1960) argue that high grievance rates may signal good relations. They contend that when operating conditions produce numerous problems and differences of opinion, and the parties feel comfortable enough in their relationship to openly express their positions, high submission rates would be anticipated.

Labig and Greer (1988) acknowledge the difficulty in drawing conclusions about the nature of a particular labor-management relationship from grievance activity alone, and, hence, recommend that greater attention be given to the type of grievances filed. According to Fossum (1989), grievances can be divided into two major categories: those that affect the job security of individual workers (e.g., discipline and discharge cases) and those that involve groups of workers (work standards and job assignments). This typology may make it easier to sort out grievances as to their cooperative potential, such as an honest disagreement over the application of contract terms, versus arbitrary treatment of workers. As a result, Labig and Greer (1988, p. 20) note that "meaningful interpretations of activity levels may be possible when type is controlled."

Even when the moderating effects of grievance type are taken into account, ambiguity remains. That is, Feuille and Wheeler (1981) claim, when grievances are used as conflict indicators, little is know about the conflict. They offer an example: "Are grievances primarily indicators of conflict between specific employees and specific managers, between the union as an organization and the employer as an organization, or between different employees competing for scarce rewards" (p. 289)? Consequently, a necessary condition for using data on grievances in describing labor-management relations is a thorough understanding of their sources and of the circumstances underlying their submission. Thus, the LMR model holds:

> Proposition 8: Grievance rates alone are insufficient when assessing the parties' relationship.

Settlement Level

Another issue that concerns the interpretation of grievances involves the level at which they should be resolved. Gordon and Miller (1984) maintain that it is in the best interests of all concerned to settle grievances at the lowest level possible in the system. Slichter et al. (1960, p. 733) cite three reasons for this practice: "(1) to maintain the authority and status of first line supervision, (2) to prevent the grievance from changing character, and (3) to gain meaningful employee acceptance."

Several factors contribute to the resolution of grievances at the lower levels of a procedure. First, in their studies, Duane (1979) and Mullen (1954) observed that many grievances were appealed to the third and fourth steps simply because lower-level management officials felt they did not have the authority to make grievance-related decisions. Davy, Stewart, and Anderson (1992) present a similar case for union stewards. They note that stewards are generally considered the key figures in the union, yet they often lack the appropriate charge to carry out their responsibilities because unions do not want these relatively low-level union officials setting precedent that may be unfavorable to the union as a whole. Implicit in these accounts is that lower level settlements occur when grievance officials are granted authority that is commensurate with their contract-administrative responsibilities.

Second, specific and unambiguous contract language promotes early resolution of grievances. Indeed, Duane (1979) found that ambiguous contract language was associated with grievance resolution at the upper levels of procedures and with uncooperative bargaining behavior. Moreover, inclusion of a contract provision that encourages early resolution of grievances has in some instances substantially reduced the number of appeals (Duane, 1990; Graham & Heshizer, 1979). Stability in operating procedures and union-management policies also encourages lower-level resolution (Slichter et al., 1960). Finally, the more mature the union-management relationship and the more experienced the first-step officials are in processing grievances, the more likely it is that grievances will be settled at this step (Duane, 1990; Bloom & Northrup, 1969). Speaking to the former condition, Bloom and Northrup (1969, p. 126) note that "once the shop foremen and the union stewards or committeemen get used to each other and to living under a contract, they are likely to work out a modus operandi." Accordingly, the LMR model prescribes:

Proposition 9: Grievances should be resolved at the lowest level possible.

CONCLUSIONS

Grievance procedures have several important effects on firm performance and labor-management relations. First, while the design of grievance procedures is fairly standardized, with a four-step process ending in arbitration being the most common, there are distinct structural variations among some labor groups and industries, including agriculture, construction, and trucking workers as well as public, nonunion, and international sectors. Second, as Table 4.3 indicates, grievance procedures tend to reduce employee turnover —"although the most recent evidence shows that knowledge of 'who prevails' in grievance settlement is critical to an understanding of the turnover consequences of grievance procedures" (Ichniowski & Lewin, 1987, p. 189). Third, productivity appears to be nonlinearly related to grievance activity, which is accounted for by divergent worker-reaction effects.

There is very little empirical research that directly assesses the effects of the grievance process on labor-management projects and contract negotiations. The evidence that is available, however,

Table 4.3
Summary of Propositions on the Relationship Between the Grievance Process and Labor-Management Outcomes

Factor	Proposition
Employee Turnover	1. Employee access to *union-type* grievance procedures reduces turnover.
Strike Activity	2. Employee access to *union-type* grievance procedures reduces wildcat strikes.
Productivity	3. Employee access to *union-type* grievance procedures increases productivity.
	4. Grievance rates are nonlinearly related to productivity.
Joint Programs	5. Employee access to *union-type* grievance procedures is a precondition for effective labor-management programs.
Contract Negotiations	6. Cooperative (hostile) grievance resolution promotes cooperative (hostile) contract negotiations.
	7. Grievance rates increase just prior to contract negotiations.
Grievance Rates	8. Grievance rates alone are insufficient when assessing the parties' relationship.
Settlement Level	9. Grievances should be resolved at the lowest level possible.

suggests that effective grievance procedures contribute to the success of joint projects and to cooperative contract negotiations—though grievance activity is expected to increase as the expiration date of the contract approaches, all things equal.

Finally, while grievance data indicate that it is in the best interests of labor and management to resolve grievances at the lowest level possible in the system, caution must be exercised in using such data in describing other intricacies of their relationship. The validity of grievance rates, as indicators of the quality of the parties' relationship, is complicated by the possibility that the meaning of the construct is different depending on the substance of particular grievances as well as the nature of the conflict. To be sure, cooperative relations are generally associated with relatively few grievances, but this is not always the case. What is suggested is that the approach the parties take in resolving grievances is a better predictor of labor-management relations and firm performance than mere grievance rates. In the following chapters, the key factors that contribute to the manner in which the parties' officials resolve grievances are discussed.

5

The Impact of Background and Boundary-Role Factors on the Grievance Process

As the LMR model indicates, the bargaining behaviors of union and management grievance officials are influenced by their background characteristics as well as by their boundary roles. The purpose of this chapter is to examine both of these potential determinants of grievance orientation.

BACKGROUND FACTORS

A fundamental assumption of industrial psychology is that variations in job performance can be predicted from the personal characteristics of workers or job applicants. A logical and natural extension of this assumption is that the bargaining orientations of grievance officials can be explained by their personal characteristics, including personality, negotiating experience, education, gender, race, and marital status.

Personality

There is extensive literature that examines the effects of personality on bargaining behavior. To illustrate, in their book *The Social*

Psychology of Bargaining and Negotiation, Jeffery Rubin and Bert Brown (1975) reviewed hundreds of studies on bargaining behavior and found that the effects of personality were the objects of considerable controversy. Indeed, they noted that in some cases, different studies of personality effects conducted by the same research team produced contradictory results. For example, in one study, Harnett and his associates (1968) found that high risk takers tended to concede less rapidly than did low risk takers. Yet in another study (1973), they found precisely the opposite relationship. The inability of these early inquiries to yield replicable findings explains why their conclusions were essentially discounted by the scientific community. Perhaps the best study of this period was one conducted by Druckman (1967), who showed that fewer concessions were made by more dogmatic negotiators, yet even this study suffers from certain methodological shortcomings.

Recent investigations in the field have attempted to improve research methodology by paying more attention to controlled experimentation. The following is a summary of the findings of these studies:

1. In a typical laboratory experiment using student subjects only 2 of the 8 personality variables—authoritarianism and self-esteem—identified differences in the way students described their own bargaining strategies, and only 2 of the 8 personality variables—cognitive complexity and self-esteem—predicted behavior choice at acceptable levels of statistical significance.
2. Only 3 of the 32 studies of personality effects on game-playing strategy approached statistical significance.
3. While certain personality variables, such as cognitive complexity, conciliatory tendency, dogmatism, risk-avoidance, and suspiciousness, did emerge as predictive personality characteristics, they did so only when subjects were matched with counterparts who scored similarly on the specific variables (Lewicki & Litterer, 1985).

As this review suggests, improvements in the research methodology generated greater consistency of results. At the same time, however, many theorists have expressed disappointment in that while isolated trends surfaced, a definitive personality effect on bargaining behavior did not. Some individuals from this camp have argued that recent studies have relied too heavily on laboratory experimentation, where ability to control is enhanced but where realism is often difficult to duplicate. But even field studies (e.g., Duane, 1984) have found no conclusive relationship between personality and negotiating behavior. Accordingly, "those who believe they are 'not the negotiating type' may be significantly misjudging the impact of their personality on attaining the desired outcomes" (Lewicki & Litterer, 1985). The LMR model, therefore, offers the following:

Proposition 1: There is no relationship between the personality characteristics of grievance officials and their bargaining behaviors.

Negotiating Experience

A cursory read of the classified ads in your favorite newspaper will reveal that jobs involving significant negotiating ability require a certain number of years' experience in the field. The assumption here is that experience in some way is related to bargaining talent. With respect to grievance negotiations, Davy et al. (1992) found that bargaining unit size and the number of grievances were positively related to grievance resolution rates prior to arbitration. They conclude that it "is possible that these two factors are proxies for experience. As individuals handle more and more grievances, they become more adept at defining the issues and understanding what it takes to reach resolution. In addition, they become more comfortable with their roles in making binding decisions that affect both the organization and the union" (p. 314).

Consistent with these observations, Purcell (1953) found that inexperienced grievance officials tended to file more grievances, many of which he judged to be without merit. Ash (1970) also observed an inverse relationship between grievance activity and the negotiating experience of those involved in the process. Labig and Greer (1988) provide indirect support for the relevance of experience by citing a study that found a significant relationship between cooperative grievance resolution and the grievance official's knowledge of bargaining unit jobs and the contract, which is typically enhanced by experience.

Similarly, Duane (1984) found that years' experience with grievance processing was positively associated with a grievance official's willingness to engage in cooperation. He explains that a cooperative approach to grievance negotiations requires the official to filter out personal differences, to focus on the problems at hand, and eventually to come up with solutions that will satisfy all those involved in the process. But the mastery of such skills generally takes time and experience. Indeed, inexperienced grievance officials may assume a hard line, not so much out of a desire for conflict but rather because it is a relatively simple means of settling disputes. After all, the adoption of firm positions on issues involves little negotiating talent and may in some cases produce short-term benefits in the form of favorable grievance settlements. Thus, the model holds:

> Proposition 2: Experience in grievance processing promotes cooperative grievance behavior.

Education

There are only two studies that have investigated the relationship between the bargaining behavior of grievance officials and their levels of education. In one, using dummy variables to represent degrees completed by officials, which ranged from bachelor's to doctoral degrees, Duane (1990) found that officials with the more advanced degrees were more predisposed to cooperate during grievance deliberations. In the other study, Bemmels, Reshef, and Stratton-Devine (1991) found that years of education of stewards and whether they completed a steward-training program did not account for variations in grievance rates. But these two education indicators were positively associated with the stewards' tendency to seek informal solutions to grievances. In other words, both studies provide evidence for a direct relationship between level of education of grievance officials and their willingness to cooperate. There is, therefore, support for the following:

> Proposition 3: Education levels of grievance officials are positively associated with cooperative grievance behavior.

Gender

Considerable research has been conducted on whether males and females differ in their bargaining behaviors. Most studies have found no difference between them (Black & Higbee, 1973; McNeel, McClintock, & Nuttin, 1972; Pruitt, 1981; Wagar & Robinson, 1989; Wyer & Malinowski, 1972). Specifically, Bemmels et al. (1991) and Duane (1984) did not detect a gender difference in bargaining orientations of grievance officials. At first glance, these findings challenge the results of early research efforts, which indicate that males bargain more aggressively than do females (Conrath, 1972; Grant & Sermat, 1969; Miller & Pyke, 1973). There are at least two ways to approach this discrepancy. First, the results of the early studies can be repudiated on the basis that they generally lack scientific rigor. Or, these results can be accepted as a genuine instance of gender difference at the time, while recognizing that social developments since then have eliminated it. Either approach, however, is consistent with the notion that male and female officials do not approach the grievance process differently. Thus, the following is proposed:

Proposition 4: There is no relationship between the gender of grievance officials and their bargaining behaviors.

Race

A few studies have analyzed the relationship between the race of workers and their proclivity to file grievances. During the early years of collective bargaining in the United States, whites tended to submit a greater proportion of grievances than did members of other racial groups (Ash, 1970; Eckerman, 1948). Studies conducted after the passage of state and federal civil-rights legislation, however, indicate no differences among races regarding grievance submission rates (Labig & Greer, 1988; Sulkin & Pranis, 1967). Thus, the LMR model holds:

Proposition 5: There is no relationship between the race of grievance officials and their bargaining behaviors.

Marital Status

When workers or union stewards take part in grievance proceedings, they always run the risk of alienating their supervisors, who, subsequently, may find ways of terminating them, even though virtually all federal and state labor laws prohibit such retaliation. And since a persuasive argument can be made that workers who have family obligations are more concerned about losing their jobs than are those who do not, one would expect more aggressive grievance action on the part of unmarried workers. But research on this particular relationship suggests that martial status does not have a significant effect on grievance-related behavior (Ash, 1970; Labig & Greer, 1988; Price, DeWire, Nowack, Schenkel, & Ronan, 1976). The model, therefore, supports the following:

Proposition 6: There is no relationship between marital status of grievance officials and their bargaining behaviors.

Summary of the Effects of Background Factors

The motives of the early scholars who examined the relationship between the background characteristics of negotiators and their bargaining behaviors were well intentioned: "It is hoped that this research will be of some help to American labor and industry in their ceaseless striving to arrive at a better understanding of their mutual problems" (Eckerman, 1948, p. 256). But, as Table 5.1 illustrates, the preponderance of the evidence indicates that only education and experience significantly explain variations in grievance orientation, with greater levels of each resulting in more cooperation. In some respects these findings are disappointing. For example, the selection process for grievance officials would have been greatly simplified if evidence had supported an association between certain personality profiles and how individuals negotiate. In other respects, the findings are welcome. Indeed, they advance equality among the sexes and races within the grievance process to the extent that these demographic factors do not account for variations in grievance orientation. The next section examines the effects of boundary-role factors on the bargaining behaviors of grievance officials.

BOUNDARY-ROLE FACTORS

Union and management grievance officials share two very different roles, which are associated with seemingly conflicting determinants of bargaining behavior. That is, as group representatives, all officials are subject to constituent expectations and demands. But they also represent the views of the other side to their constituents, and in doing so, they are likely to be familiar with the other side's priorities, strengths, weaknesses, and predilections. With this special knowledge, officials are likely to alter how they

Table 5.1
Summary of Propositions on the Effects of Background Factors

Factor	Proposition
Personality	1. There is no relationship between the personality characteristics of grievance officials and their bargaining behaviors.
Experience	2. Experience in grievance processing promotes cooperative grievance behavior.
Education	3. Education levels of grievance officials are positively associated with cooperative grievance behavior.
Gender	4. There is no relationship between the gender of grievance officials and their bargaining behaviors.
Race	5. There is no relationship between the race of grievance officials and their bargaining behaviors.
Marital Status	6. There is no relationship between marital status of grievance officials and their bargaining behaviors.

approach grievances, which may be reflected in their bargaining orientations. These potential determinants of grievance behavior are often referred to as "boundary-role" factors (Druckman, 1967; Wall & Adams, 1974). Discussion of these factors will be separated into two groups: those factors that involve constituent demands and those that are related to the grievance officials' relationship.

Constituent Demands

Pfeffer (1982) argues that the behavior of group or organizational representatives is severely constrained by perceptions of how their constituents want them to perform. As representatives, most grievance officials are at least somewhat interested in pleasing their constituents, primarily because it is assumed that they must do so in order to remain in their positions. Pruitt (1981, p. 42) notes that representatives who are normally predisposed to cooperate, but whose constituents stress aggression, will "usually be less conciliatory than those who are negotiating on their own behalf. They will concede more slowly, reach fewer agreements, and take more time to reach agreement." In a laboratory experiment conducted by Benton and Druckman (1974), the bargaining behaviors of subjects were observed, some of whom had information about constituent demands and expectations, while the others did not. Their results suggest that the subjects' bargaining orientations were partially driven by constituent wishes, whether they were to stress compromise, cooperation, or aggression. Moreover, a field study of public-sector grievance officials found that they were more assertive in their bargaining demands when their constituents were perceived as being hostile to the other party (Duane, 1991b).

Further support for the effects of constituent demands on the behaviors of negotiators comes from Pruitt (1981), who suggests that representatives try even harder to please their constituents when they are either highly accountable to them or subject to intense surveillance by them. In their studies, Gruder (1971) and Klimoski and Ash (1974) also observed that the bargaining orientations of subjects were more closely aligned with the wishes of their constituents when they had access to information about the outcomes of negotiations. Finally, Organ (1971) reports that subjects in a laboratory experiment were more likely to conform to the instructions given them by their constituents when they could easily observe the subjects' behaviors.

A fascinating corollary is that when representatives have little or mixed information about their constituents' expectations or desires, their negotiating approach is typically more aggressive than if they were negotiating on their own behalf (Benton, 1972; Benton & Druckman, 1973; Druckman, Solomon & Zechmeister, 1972; Pruitt, 1981). This suggests that, all things equal, representatives assume that their constituents want them to be tough and aggressive in negotiations. And to the extent that it may take some time for representatives to fully comprehend the desires of their constituents, this explanation is compatible with the fact that novice negotiators bargain more aggressively than do more experienced ones. Hence, the LMR model proposes the following:

Proposition 1: Cooperative (hostile) constituent expectations are associated with cooperation (hostility) by grievance officials, particularly when they are held highly accountable or when they are open to surveillance by their constituents.

Proposition 2: With little or mixed information about constituent expectations, grievance officials are less likely to cooperate.

Within the context of collective bargaining, the attitudes and politics of both parties provide unique boundary-role constraints: union attitudes and policies as well as management attitudes and policies.

Union Attitudes and Policies. Several researchers have examined how union attitudes toward management affect the grievance process. Glassman and Belasco (1975), for example, found that positive, friendly attitudes regarding management were related to fewer grievances. But, more importantly they observed that the best predictor of variations in grievance rates was how rank-and-file workers felt about joint decision-making. Their findings suggest that grievance rates are highest among union members who believe in joint decision-making, but where management is unwilling to share its authority with them.

With respect to a steward's commitment to the company, Dalton and Todor (1982) indicate that it has a positive effect on cooperative grievance behavior, as measured by attempts to discourage workers from filing grievances, and the steward's willingness to settle grievances informally. Conversely, a steward's commitment to the union was found to have a significant direct impact on grievance rates and on a steward's encouragement to file grievances (Bemmels et al., 1991).

The policies of the union generally and of the union grievance official in particular are obviously salient to the grievance process. The results of studies by Duane (1984) and Bemmels et al. (1991), for example, suggest that when a union grievance official has a policy of approaching labor-management problems informally (i.e., attempting to settle potential grievances by discussing the problems with management), fewer grievances are filed, and those that are filed tend to be resolved to the mutual satisfaction of both parties. Bemmels et al. (1991) also note an important interaction effect between a union grievance official's policy of informal problem resolution and a manager's knowledge of the bargaining agreement. That is, when management officials are unfamiliar with the agreement, the effect of informal problem resolution on reducing grievance rates is enhanced. Bemmels et al. contend (p., 23):

> A likely interpretation of this positive interaction is that attempts at informal grievance resolution by the stewards are often successful if the supervisor has little knowledge of the collective agreement. In this situation the steward may be able to resolve the problem by simply pointing out provisions of the agreement that the supervisor did not know about. If, however, the supervisor is already well aware of the provisions in the collective agreement, but, for whatever reason, chooses to ignore those provisions, attempts at informal resolution may be more difficult.

Union politics also influence the bargaining orientations of union stewards. To illustrate, union officers, who are up for reelection or are members of a union that is being challenged by another labor organization for the right to represent bargaining unit members, often encourage stewards to file grievances (Begin, 1971; Labig & Greer, 1988; Peach & Livernash, 1974; Slichter et al., 1960). The primary objective here is to demonstrate to their members that the current union administration is actively working to protect their rights. In some cases, however, this strategy has backfired. For instance, in their study of union rivalry at International Harvester, McKersie and Shropshire (1965) noticed that the number of grievances filed during this period increased to a point where the entire system broke down, which eventually resulted in unit dissatisfaction with settlements.

Similarly, grievance rates are likely to increase just prior to new contract negotiations. The explanation for this is twofold. First, workers may submit more grievances at this point to remind the union negotiating team of issues that are important to them. Second, union officials may encourage unit members to file grievances in order to send signals to management concerning priority bargaining issues as well as to build solidarity among their membership, particularly when economic action is anticipated. This discussion supports a series of propositions:

Proposition 3: Positive opinions of management promote cooperative behavior by the union grievance official.

Proposition 4: When the union grievance official is committed to the firm (union), that person is more (less) likely to cooperate.

Proposition 5: A union policy of approaching labor-management problems informally promotes cooperative behavior by the union grievance official.

Proposition 6: Officer elections, union rivalry, and preparations for contract negotiations produce higher grievance rates and less cooperation by the union grievance official.

Management Attitudes and Politics. The effects of management attitudes on the grievance process are somewhat more difficult to assess, since management rarely initiates grievances. Fleishman and Harris (1962), however, found interesting interacting effects regarding management concern for workers and the design of their jobs, whether their structure was high or low, on grievance rates. That is, grievance rates were not significantly affected by high levels of consideration and low job structure. But low levels of consideration and high job structure were positively associated with greivance rates. In support of these findings, Peach and Livernash (1974) observed that inactive and autocratic foremen provoked more grievances than did managers who tended to be problem solvers. They note further that one of the major differences between departments with high grievance and those with low rates was in management's policy regarding consultation with the union. Specifically, "consultation did tend to reduce the formal grievance rate since it was conducive to informal resolution. When the union was consulted beforehand, the likelihood that union leaders would instigate or support a challenge to the decision decreased markedly" (pp. 113–114). The importance of consultation with the union in reducing grievance rates has been addressed by several scholars (Dean, 1954; Fleming & Witte, 1959; Gandz, 1979; Kaplan, 1950; Labig & Greer, 1988; Whyte, 1967). They argue that this effect occurs for a variety of reasons: (1) it helps to overcome resistance to change, (2) it assists the parties in developing procedures that are satisfactory to workers, and (3) it reduces union defensiveness.

Slichter et al. (1960) point out that management can choose from at least three discrete grivance-handling policies, each of which has a different impact on the grievance processs. First, management may adopt a policy of taking a firm stand on grievances, without regard to the union's position or eventual response. This policy produces varying levels of grievance rates. That is, when it is initially adopted the number of grievances increases, but over time the refusal of management to listen to union arguments or to yield to threats of economic pressure discourages workers from filing grievances, even when they involve complaints for which they have strong feelings. Second, management may adopt a policy of taking a reasonable, carefully analyzed stand on grievances, while acquiescing to the union in the face of economic pressure. Needless to say, this policy invites protests and complaints. As a result, it produces high grievance rates. Finally, management may adopt a policy of taking a reasonable, carefully analyzed stand on grievances, and sticking firmly to it even in the face of economic pressure. Unlike the first policy option, this one does not preclude management from listening to union arguments and even changing its stand if convinced by the union's facts or logic. Still, "there is a vital difference between listening to arguments and yielding to economic pressure, such as slowdowns, refusal to work overtime and wildcat strikes" (Slichter et al.,1960, p. 717). This policy of being fair yet firm usually produces low grievance rates as well as cooperative grievance resolution. The LMR model, therefore, includes:

Proposition 7: When low levels of management consideration for workers is accompanied by high job structure, the grievance official is less likely to cooperate.

Proposition 8: A management policy of consulting the union regarding labor-management problems is associated with cooperative behavior by the grievance management official.

Proposition 9: A management policy of not engaging in joint decision-making with union members is associated with uncooperative behavior by the management grievance official.

Proposition 10: A management policy of assuming a firm stand on greivances, regardless of the union's position, is associated with uncooperative behavior by the management grievance official.

Proposition 11: A management policy of assuming a firm stand on grievances, while taking into account union arguments and positions, is associated with cooperative behavior by the management official.

The Grievance Officials' Relationship

While constituent demands and expectations are important determinants of the bargaining behaviors of grievance officials, just as influential perhaps is their other set of boundary-role factors, involving their relationship with each other. It is well known, for example, that cooperation is more likely among individuals who can identify with one another (Hornstein, 1976). In summarizing the literature in this area, Staub, (1978, p. 113) makes the comment that "when we define people as 'we,'we are more likely to help them." There is similar evidence that people are more cooperative with individuals whom they like (Baron, 1971), with whom they can empathize (Coke, Batson & McDavis, 1978) and who have some control over the individuals' future benefits (Pruitt, 1968; 1981). Duane (1991b, p. 88) found that social interactions between the grievance officials fostered cooperation, as the following account illustrates:

> Bob (management representative) and I are pretty good friends. In fact, we go fishing each summer for a couple of weeks right before school starts. . . . We often discuss the problems that face teachers and staff at school, and he seems to be very responsive to them. Perhaps that's why we haven't had to file any grievances against him since he became principal here.

Some bargaining experiments have been conducted to assess the effects of the quality of the relationship between negotiators in general on their bargaining behaviors. For example, in their negotiation exercise, Fry, Firestone, and Williams (1979) observed that more rapid concessions were made within dating couples than within matched subjects who were strangers to each each. In another bargaining game, Mullick and Lewis (1977) found that subjects who cared more for their mates conceded more to them than did other male companions. In short, these findings suggest that friendly feelings between negotiators generally and between grievance officials specifically increase their propensity to cooperate.

Another important dynamic of the officials' relationship is perceived intention of the other side. For example, Gruder (1971) notes that negotiators tend to acquiesce more rapidly to their counterparts when they are perceived to be cooperatively predisposed. More specifically, Komorita and Esser (1975) and Pruitt (1981) argue that negotiators are more inclined to cooperate when they view the other as *both firm and fair*. When the other is viewed as *firm but not fair,* negotiators are not likely to cooperate out of fear that the other will mismatch their orientation. When the other is viewed as *fair but not firm,* negotiators are likely to adopt a hostile or uncooperative orientation. Pruitt (1981, p. 38) adds that a bargainer's "perception that the other party is being cooperative, and hence the bargainer's likelihood of reciprocating the other's concessions, will probably be strengthened by any evidence that these concessions are voluntary and internally motivated rather than accidental or pressed on the other by external circumstances."

An obvious source of information available to a negotiator concerning the intentions of the other party is that person's observable behavior (Duane, Azevedo, & Anderson, 1985). In her famous treatise *Intention,* Anscombe (1957, p. 8) argues that "if you want to say at least some true things about a man's intentions, you will have a strong chance of success if you mention what he actually did or is doing." The prudent negotiator, however, understands that an opponent may be motivated to generate misleading impressions of intent by, for example, appearing to be accommodative in an effort to gain the negotiator's trust, only to violate it later.

Results from a field study by Duane et al. (1985) indicate that grievance officials were able to identify the intentions of their counterparts from their bargaining behaviors only when these behaviors were of an extreme nature, either very cooperative or very hostile. This observation is consistent with the attribution theorists' notion of probable cause, which accounts for the tendency of individuals to misattribute moderate behavior (Duval & Duval, 1983; Nisbett & Schachter, 1966; Singerman, Barkovec &

Baron, 1976). But why are extreme behaviors such accurate signals of a counterpart's intentions? Duane et al. (1985) argue that the ability of grievance officials to correctly attribute extreme bargaining behaviors is due largely to the fact that such action involves overt downside risks. That is, extreme cooperative behaviors in the form of an open exchange of priorities, values, and financial data are highly susceptible to exploitation; hence, they are not likely to be exhibited unless the counterpart truly intends to engage in cooperation. Likewise, extreme hostile behaviors, such as firm positional commitments and an unwillingness to legitimately consider alternative solutions to problems, have at least a chilling effect on interparty communication and, thus, are likely to be displayed only when the negotiator is truly uninterested in cooperation.

It is therefore this readiness to accept the downside risk associated with extreme bargaining behaviors that enhances accuracy of attribution. This conclusion should be of value to grievance officials in that it suggests that when a counterpart exhibits extreme behaviors, they can safely assume that these behaviors reflect the person's true intentions, making it easier for them to devise an appropriate response. On the other hand, when confronted by a counterpart who displays moderate bargaining behavior (e.g., a willingness to split the difference), misattribution is possible. To assess that person's true intent, therefore, the official must gather more information. Braver and Barnett (1976), for example, suggest that observing another's behavior with a third party may provide instructive cues of intent. Thus the LMR model includes:

Proposition 12: Friendly relations between the grievance officials are associated with cooperation between them.

Proposition 13: Expectations of continued interactions with a counterpart are associated with cooperative behavior by the grievance official.

Table 5.2
Summary of Propositions on the Effects of Boundary-Role Factors

Factor	Proposition
Constituent Demands (General)	1. Cooperative (hostile) constituent expectations are associated with cooperation (hostility) by grievance officials, particularly when they are held highly accountable or when they are open to surveillance by their constituents.
	2. With little or mixed information about constituent expectations, grievance officials are less likely to cooperate.
Constituent Demands (Union)	3. Positive opinions of management promote cooperative behavior by the union grievance official.
	4. When the union grievance official is committed to the firm (union), that person is more (less) likely to cooperate.
	5. A union policy of approaching labor-management problems informally promotes cooperative behavior by the union grievance official.
	6. Officer elections, union rivalry, and preparations for contract negotiations produce higher grievance rates and less cooperation by the union grievance official.
Constituent Demands (Management)	7. When low levels of management consideration for workers is accompanied by high job structure, the grievance official is less likely to cooperate.
	8. A management policy of consulting the union regarding labor-management problems is associated with cooperative behavior by the management grievance official.

Proposition 14: When a counterpart is viewed as both firm and fair, the grievance official is more likely to cooperate.

Proposition 15: When a counterpart is viewed as firm but not fair, the grievance official is less likely to cooperate.

Table 5.2 (Continued)

Factor	Proposition
	9. A management policy of not engaging in joint decision-making with union members is associated with uncooperative behavior by the management grievance official.
	10. A management policy of assuming a firm stand on grievances, regardless of the union's position, is associated with uncooperative behavior by the management grievance official.
	11. A management policy of taking a firm stand on grievances, while taking into account union arguments and positions, is associated with cooperative behavior by the management grievance official.
Officials' Relationship	12. Friendly relations between the officials are associated with cooperation between them.
	13. Expectations of continued interactions with a counterpart are associated with cooperative behavior by the grievance official.
	14. When a counterpart is viewed as both firm and fair, the grievance official is more likely to cooperate.
	15. When a counterpart is viewed as firm but not fair, the grievance official is less likely to cooperate.
	16. When a counterpart is viewed as fair but not firm, the grievance official is less likely to cooperate.
	17. Extreme cooperative (hostile) bargaining behaviors by a counterpart serve as accurate indicators of that person's bargaining intentions.

Proposition 16: When a counterpart is viewed as fair but not firm, the grievance official is less likely to cooperate.

Proposition 17: Extreme cooperative (hostile) bargaining behaviors by a counterpart serve as accurate indicators of that person's bargaining intentions.

Summary of the Effects of Boundary-Role Factors

As Table 5.2 indicates, the behavior of grievance officials is constrained by the fact that they must be responsive to the interests of their constituents, while being somewhat interested in responding to the needs of their counterparts. Indeed, an official's constituents may establish boundary-role safeguards to ensure compliance with their wishes. They may, for example, hold the official highly accountable for the number of grievances filed and their outcomes. A further safeguard is for the constituents to monitor closely the actions of their official during grievance negotiations. One way to do this is to add another member of their group to the grievance negotiation process.

Obviously, the grievance official's relationship is critical in defining the quality of their deliberations. It is widely assumed, for example, that the way a counterpart approaches these deliberations has a tremendous impact on a grievance official's bargaining orientation. The hope here is that the official's reaction is appropriate. To aid the official in this endeavor, it is submitted that extreme counterpart behaviors serve as reliable indicators of a counterpart's intent, but that misattribution may occur from moderate behaviors without further related information. An important source of such information comes from the bargaining environment, which will be discussed in the next chapter.

6

The Impact of Environmental Factors on the Grievance Process

Grievance negotiations do not occur in a vacuum. There are, in fact, several forces at work here, often referred to as environmental factors: economic conditions, technology, legal regulations, bargaining setting, and the collective bargaining agreement. The purpose of this chapter is to evaluate the effects of these environmental factors on the grievance process, with particular emphasis on how they affect the behaviors of grievance officials.

ECONOMIC CONDITIONS

While little solid research has been conducted on the impact of economic conditions on the grievance process, considerable attention has been paid to their effects on strikes. And since strikes and grievances are often equated as measures of worker discontent with management, one would expect that they would respond similarly to changes in economic conditions. In support of this tenet, Kochan (1980) notes that studies of the causes of strikes generally, and wildcat strikes in particular, have focused on the same set of environmental factors as those that are used in grievance activity. It is hoped, therefore, that an analysis of the impact of economic factors on strikes will provide some insight into how the grievance process functions.

There has been a general decline in the number of strikes over the past few decades, to a point where the 1980s and 1990s witnessed very few of them. Still, the number of strikes fluctuate greatly from year to year, suggesting that changes in institutional, political, and economic circumstances make a difference. But as Kaufman (1986) notes, the single most important influence on the level of strike activity in the post-World War II period has been the variation in economic activity over the business cycle. He maintains that "the typical pattern is for strike activity to be *procyclical*, increasing on the upswing of the business cycle and falling off on the downswing. The major explanation for this pattern is the impact that changes in inflation and unemployment have on bargaining" (p. 487).

Periods of high inflation—for example, after World Wars I and II, during the Korean War, through the years of the Vietnam War, as well as those succeeding years—have resulted in elevated strike levels (Chamberlain & Kuhn, 1986). Studies have also found a strong negative link between the unemployment rate and the number of strikes. Tying grievance activity to this link, A. Rees (1952) comments that when the unemployment rate is high, the balance of power tips in management's favor, causing the union to store up its grievances rather than take risks on potentially disastrous strikes. Finally, strike activity appears to correlate negatively with management predictability of environmental conditions, as measured by an employer's ease in access to supplier markets (Cousineau & LaCroix, 1986). The LMR model, therefore, supports the following propositions:

Proposition 1: Inflation is positively related to grievance rates.

Proposition 2: Unemployment rates are inversely related to grievance rates.

Proposition 3: Management predictability of environmental conditions is inversely related to grievance rates.

TECHNOLOGY

Technology refers to the instruments and methods used in the production processes and in the handling of materials. The effects of technology on the grievance process have been extensively analyzed. Kuhn (1961) compared the grievance activity in four large tire plants with the activity in large electrical equipment plants. He found that grievance rates were higher in plants where the technology: (1) required substantive interactions among workers, (2) encouraged individualized work pace, and (3) promoted the specialization of jobs. In their comparison of departments with high and low grievance rates, Peach and Livernash (1974) revealed that the technology in high-rate departments: (1) required greater worker attention, (2) required greater worker responsibility for production output, and (3) involved more individualized work assignments. Inasmuch as these studies were of large manufacturing facilities only, one must be cautious in applying their findings to other organizational settings.

Labig and Greer's (1988) review of the early research in this area cuts across organizational and industry divisions, and it discloses some common findings. They note, for example, that grievance activity is positively related to three technological factors: (1) worker control of output, (2) work variability (or change in work methods), and (3) work essential to the rest of the plant. Conversely, "required coordination among workers is negatively related to grievance activity" (p. 7).

Recent technological innovations have had dramatic effects on industrial relations. They have helped to determine the types of jobs available, while promoting productivity, safer working conditions, and higher standards of living. Robotics, for example, has been used to relieve workers of having to perform dangerous tasks typically associated with forging, foundry work, tool loading, and hazardous-materials handling, thereby reducing workers' compensation costs, employee absenteeism, and litigation from occupational injuries and illnesses (Holley & Jennings, 1988).

To say that these technological innovations have not been wholeheartedly supported by the labor movement is an understatement by anyone's measure. Indeed, Joseph Konowe (1983, p. A-3), a Teamster official, called robots "steel-collar workers" who "do not belong to the union, do not need sick leave, vacation, coffee breaks, cost-of-living increases, etc., and will work around the clock with nary a thought of overtime pay." His comments accentuate the workers' dismay with shifts in technology, if not their outright fear of them, as threats to their work assignments, pay levels, and, most important, job security. According to Slichter et al., (1960, p. 706), "periods of change in methods of operation thus are likely to produce grievances." In the 1960s, for example, employers in the maritime industry wanted to introduce technological change. When the West Coast dockworkers got wind of this plan, they initiated grievances, expressing their concerns about the potential loss of jobs. The parties eventually worked out an agreement whereby the dockworkers would receive permanent job security in exchange for their cooperation in the implementation of the cost-saving technology.

Union officials have approached new technologies cautiously. Full cooperation with management, on the one hand, is likely to be perceived by union members and other unions as a violation of the responsibilities of the union to represent the interests of its membership. Yet, by maintaining a distance, union officials run the risk of dealing with technological change as a fait accompli. Their task is further complicated by the fact that job displacement cannot be tied easily to specific changes in technology and may often by disguised by shifts in product mix or sourcing strategies. Thus, unions have tended to focus on how technological change affects job content as well as on the process by which management introduces such change. R. Thomas (1991, p. 183) provides a splendid illustration of this policy:

> The union, which had not been informed of the impending arrival of the CNC [computer numerical control] equipment by either management or the designated machine operators, filed an inquiry nearly as soon as the machines were bolted down. An extensive discussion with several shop stewards revealed two underlying concerns. The first was traditional: the new equipment altered the way operators worked (e.g., requiring them to manually input data) and the additional tasks seemed to warrant an increase in pay and, perhaps a change in job classification. They felt that the existing classification (NC machine operator) was inappropriate for the job since other workers with similar classifications were not trained to run the machines. The second concern was more complicated. The stewards argued that introducing the equipment without advance notification undermined the spirit of the new technology agreement by keeping the process invisible and secretive. Advance consultation and training for the employees involved were applauded, but the stewards argued that consulting with employees without prior (or simultaneous) consultation with the union could introduce inequities. As one steward suggested, management could assign a new machine as a reward for compliance from "favored" workers. Regarding an employee with a new machine or a higher-status assignment could, from the union's perspective, engender divisiveness among employees.

This case analysis suggests that technological change that either alters the content of bargaining-unit jobs, without appropriated adjustments to pay or job classification, or that has not involved input from unions will have a negative effect on union-management relations, as manifest by an increase in grievances and a less cooperative approach to their resolution. Thus, the LMR model offers three propositions regarding technology:

Proposition 4: Technology that enhances worker control over output and work variability, and that makes the job more essential to the rest of the plant, is associated with higher grievance rates.

Proposition 5: Technological change without union input is associated with higher grievance rates and less cooperative grievance behavior by union officials.

Proposition 6: Technological change that alters job content without appropriate pay and classification adjustments is associated with higher grievance rates and less cooperative grievance behavior by union officials.

LEGAL REGULATIONS

The evolution of labor legislation and its interpretation by the courts and the NLRB have substantially shaped the way labor and management resolve their disputes. To illustrate, Section 9(a) of the NLRA states that "any individual employee or a group of employees shall have the right at any time to present grievances to their employers." For years, the NLRB had no occasion to render an interpretation of this portion of the law. But during World War II, the North American Aviation Company believed that the law gave employees the right to file grievances individually regardless of the existence of a collective bargaining agreement. The NLRB initially ruled against the employer but, upon appeal, a federal court reversed the decision. Taylor and Witney (1987, p. 425) comment:

> Beyond reversing the Board's decision, the court's ruling stimulated the first formal NLRB interpretation of the grievance provision. In general, the Board's General Counsel took the position that the provision meant that an individual employee had the technical right to present grievances to an

> employer, but that a representative of the certified union must be present each time an employee makes such a presentation, and must negotiate the settlement of the grievance.

In 1947 the Taft-Hartley Act amended the grievance provision. Under the new terms, grievance procedures had to meet the following standards: (1) an employee must be allowed to present grievances on an individual basis, (2) an employer must allow a union official to be present during the deliberations over grievances, and (3) an employer must be permitted to adjust such grievances with individual employees or union representatives, provided that their resolutions are consistent with a legally negotiated collective bargaining agreement. The first two standards did little to modify the grievance process. Previously, employees were allowed to present their own grievances, and unions were allowed to attend hearings dealing with grievances; indeed, they had the exclusive right to negotiate their settlements. It was only in those cases, where the union refused to participate in the resolution of grievances, that employees could individually negotiate with their employers.

The third standard, however, challenged the collective bargaining process itself. By providing that employers could negotiate grievance settlements with individual employees, this standard rescinded the exclusive right of unions to negotiate grievances, thereby weakening the principle of collective representation by labor organizations. But as Taylor and Witney (1987, p. 427) note, "any adjustment made through this arrangement since the Taft-Hartley enactment must be consistent with the terms of an existing collective bargaining contract. If individuals were permitted to reach agreements inconsistent with the contract, the entire process of collective bargaining would disintegrate rapidly."

As the law stands, unions are obligated to provide fair and impartial treatment to bargaining-unit members who request grievance representation, regardless of whether or not they belong to the union. But unions do not have to process every grievance that is brought to them. This issue was raised in an incident where two steelworkers were suspended for fighting on the job, one for 25 days and the other for 4 days. While acknowledging that the workers did deserve some discipline for their violations, the union felt that the former worker had been unfairly treated and thus filed a grievance, which eventually led to a reduction of the suspension from 25 to 14 days. At the same time, the union refused to process a grievance for the other employee, who then filed a complaint against the union. The NLRB ruled that the union did not violate its statutory duties by attempting to equalize the penalties (*United Steelworkers of America,* 225 NLRB 54, 1976).

Despite this 1976 NLRB ruling, many unions continued to be sensitive to charges of breach of duty of fair representation; as a result, they frequently processed trivial grievances, and even those that were devoid of any merit. In 1979, however, the NLRB issued guidelines for appraising complaints against unions charged with failure to properly process grievances. They indicate that measures will be taken only if the union conduct was based on improper motives, such as fraud, arbitrariness, or gross negligence; or was critical in improperly undercutting an employee's grievance (National Labor Relations Board, 1979). These guidelines have made it easier for union officials to be more selective in pursuing employee complaints, and in this way they have reduced grievance rates and increased the potential for cooperative grievance negotiations.

As noted earlier, most union grievance procedures end in arbitration. Grievance or rights arbitration has been the subject of considerable court action. In its *Lincoln Mills* decision, the U.S. Supreme Court ruled that one party could legally sue the other for refusing to arbitrate a labor dispute (*Textile Workers Union v. Lincoln Mills*, 1957). The practical implication of this decision is that when a bargaining agreement stipulates that arbitration must be used to resolve grievance disputes, the employer must proceed to arbitration. Should the employer refuse, a federal court can force arbitration through an injunction. Three years later, citing *Lincoln Mills* as precedent, the Court issued decisions in three Steelworkers cases, commonly referred to as the "Steelworkers Trilogy." The first case (*United Steelworkers v. American Manufacturing Co*., 1960), involved a grievance over reinstatement of an employee to his job after it was determined that he was 25 percent disabled. The lower court agreed with the employer, proclaiming that the employee's grievance was "a frivolous, patently baseless one, not subject to arbitration." In its decision, the Court overruled the lower court, by holding that federal courts have limited authority in determining what is arbitrable, but have no authority in evaluating the merits of a grievance.

In the second case (*United Steelworkers v. Warrior Gulf Navigation Co.*, 1960), the Court held that in the absence of a specific statement excluding arbitration, the parties would be directed to arbitrate grievances. Put somewhat differently, "the Court would not find a case nonarbitrable unless the parties specifically excluded a subject from the arbitration process" (Taylor & Witney, 1987, p. 442). This decision demonstrated the importance of arbitration as "the substitute for industrial strife." Writing for the majority, Justice William O. Douglas held:

> The collective bargaining agreement states the rights and duties of the parties. It is more than a contract; it is a generalized code to govern myriad cases which the draftsmen cannot wholly anticipate. . . . Arbitration is a means of solving the unforeseeable by making a system of private law for all the problems which may arise and to provide for their solution in a way which will generally accord with the variant needs and desires of the parties. . . . Apart from matters that the parties specifically exclude, all of the questions on which the parties disagree must therefore come within the scope of the grievance and arbitration provisions of the collective bargaining agreement.

The third case of the trilogy (*United Steelworkers v. Enterprise Wheel and Car Corp.*, 1960) further accentuated the role of arbitration in the collective bargaining process. The facts of the case involved the discharge of several employees who were protesting the firing of another employee. The discharges were eventually appealed to an arbitrator, who directed the employer to reinstate some of the employees and to pay them back wages. The case was complicated by the fact that the award was rendered five days after the contract expired, which led a lower court to rule that the arbitrator's award was unenforceable. In the end, the Court reversed the lower court and ordered full compliance with the arbitrator's decision. Again, Justice Douglas stated:

> Interpretation of the collective bargaining agreement is a question for the arbitrator. It is the arbitrator's construction which was bargained for; and so far as the arbitration decision concerns construction of the contract, the courts have no business overruling him because their interpretation of the contract is different from his. . . . The refusal of courts to review the merits of an arbitrator's award is the proper approach to arbitration under collective agreements. The federal policy of settling labor disputes would be undermined if the courts had the final say on the merits of the awards.

These decisions do not preclude the courts from reviewing arbitration cases that involve allegations of procedural misconduct, such as decisions that are obtained by arbitrary or capricious treatment, or that violate federal statutes. Aside from these exceptions, the Steelworkers Trilogy makes it all too clear that the parties may not use the courts to circumvent arbitration, or to overturn an arbitrator's award.

Perhaps at no other moment in history has the Court's integrity been called into question more than when it issued conflicting decisions over the arbitration of no-strike clauses. In the first case (*Sinclair Refining Co. v. Atkinson*, 1962) the Court, citing the Norris-LaGuardia Act of 1932, refused to enjoin a strike that occurred during the life of a contract, even though it contained a no-strike provision along with a grievance procedure, ending in arbitration. But in 1970 the Court insisted that this decision was "a significant departure from our otherwise consistent emphasis upon the Congressional policy to promote the peaceful settlement of labor disputes through arbitration." Accordingly, it reversed itself in its *Boys Markets* decision. Specifically, the Court held that under a no-strike agreement, a strike could be enjoined if a union refused to arbitrate a dispute when the company was willing to do so (*Boys Markets, Inc. v. Retail Clerks*, 1970).

While the *Boys Markets* decision may have made sense in that it discouraged strikes over grievances when arbitration was available, it received harsh criticism from the U.S. Congress, which had not altered its policy. This reaction was reflected in the following excerpt from the *Wall Street Journal* (1970):

> As a matter of fact, such legislation was introduced, but Congress so far has not seen fit to act. Congressional action, of course, would have been much the better way. However desirable the result, the Supreme Court still should restrain itself from assuming the tasks that properly belong to the legislators.

Following the *Boys Markets* decision, it was assumed that unions would be reluctant to negotiate no-strike provisions. Indeed, under this decision, employers could not obtain injunctions to stop strikes unless no-strike and arbitration clauses were part of the bargaining agreement. Yet, as Taylor and Witney (1987, p. 452) observe, "these speculations were not realized. There is no evidence that contracts now contain fewer no-strike and arbitration clauses than they did before *Boys Markets*."

Recent Court decisions both modify and reaffirm their previous rulings. In one case (*AT&T Technologies, Inc. v. Communications Workers of America*, 1986), the parties could not agree on whether certain disputes were subject to arbitration. The Court directed lower courts to rule on the arbitrability of these disputes. Without question, the Court strayed from its previous position, which bestowed "this authority on arbitrators. But as Fossum (1989, p. 401) notes, "this does not mean an arbitrator cannot rule on arbitrability, but the decision would be subject to court review, and, if a dispute existed, one of the parties could petition the courts to decide arbitrability before the case was heard."

In another case (*United Paperworkers International Union v. Misco, Inc.*, 1987) an employee was arrested and subsequently fired for smoking marijuana in the company parking lot. A grievance was submitted and eventually decided by an arbitrator, who reinstated the employee. The company appealed the decision, and while the federal district court upheld the arbitrator, the circuit court of appeals reversed the decision on the basis that it was inconsistent with public policy on drug use. In its decision, the Court agreed with the arbitrator and indicated that "in the absence of fraud or dishonesty, courts may not review a decision on its" merits, or for errors of fact, or possible contract misinterpretations." It also specified that courts could overturn awards on the basis of public policy only if "the policy is well defined, dominates the interests of the employee or employers, and has a history of laws and legal precedents to support it."

By and large, the courts and the NLRB have issued decisions that promote cooperative grievance negotiations. And in so doing, they have been true to the letter and spirit of the emerging labor legislation. To illustrate, the Title IV amendment to the NLRA established a Joint Committee on Labor-Management Relations, whose primary charge is to investigate and report on the "basic problems *affecting friendly labor relations* and productivity" [emphasis added]. The ultimate goal of this committee is to reach "consensus on policy recommendations for interpretation or modification of the laws so that they support both the ingredients and the goals of labor-management cooperation rather than conflict with them" (Schlossberg & Fetter, 1986, pp. 1–2). Therefore, the evidence surrounding the effects of legal regulations on the grievance process supports the following propositions:

Proposition 7: The courts and the NLRB discourage the submission of grievances that are frivolous or devoid of merit, thereby reducing grievance rates, while promoting cooperative bargaining behavior by both grievance officials.

Proposition 8: Labor laws, along with the courts' and NLRB's interpretations of them, encourage the parties to resolve their differences jointly through the grievance process, rather than by strikes or lockouts, or other adversarial dispute-resolution mechanisms.

BARGAINING SETTING

In 1951 an argument arose over the movement of the Korean cease-fire negotiations from Kaesong to Panmunjom. In 1978 it was decided that Camp David would provide a sufficiently neutral site for negotiations over an Israeli-Egyptian accord. And in 1991 the location of contact talks between the UAW and Caterpillar was hotly contested. These are but a few examples of where the bargaining setting has been an issue. Indeed, negotiators generally agree that one of the most important prebargaining considerations is where the negotiations will be held.

One of the major benefits of holding negotiations on one's home turf is control over the bargaining setting (Duane, Azevedo & Rhee, 1987; Martindale, 1971; Lewicki & Litterer, 1985; Rubin & Brown, 1975). Hosts do have better access to information and support services than do visiting negotiators. They are also able to arrange the physical environment to their advantage; to sit behind their own desks; to be interrupted, if desired; and to schedule bargaining sessions at a time and date to suit their own preferences. Rubin and Brown (1975, p. 82) note:

> A bargainer who views himself as having higher status than his opponent may seek control over the bargaining site in order to arrange it in a manner that both affirms his superiority and is likely to induce deference from the other. Conversely,

a bargainer having subordinate status may attempt to arrange the site in a way that offsets the status differential.

An interesting by-product of greater control over the bargaining site is increased cooperation by the host. To illustrate, Duane et al. (1987) observed that grievance officials tended to be more accommodative when negotiations were held on their own turf rather than on neutral territory or at an opponent's office. There are three reasons why this occurs. First, the social norms of politeness ingrained in many of us dictate it is rude to be hostile to guests. Second, host negotiators are more familiar with their surroundings, making them less defensive and guarded than visiting negotiators. Fisher and Ury (1981, p. 141) argue that negotiators who meet on the other's turf are, for whatever reason, suspicious of the surroundings, "aware that the setting might have been deliberately designed to make you want to conclude negotiations promptly and, if necessary, to yield points in order to do so." Third, since host negotiators feel more secure in their own environment, they are likely to be more responsive to the concerns of their visitors.

In the following, Duane et al. (1987, p. 380) provide an account that illustrates this point: "Bill [the management grievance official] always seems more at ease when we hold our negotiations at his office. We seem to be able to work out a more favorable deal [for both of us] there, than anywhere else." In short, Fisher and Ury (1981) recommend that it is sometimes advantageous to accept an offer to meet on the other side's turf. It may put them at ease, making them more open to your suggestions and more predisposed to cooperate with you.

The site of grievance negotiations also has important implications for third-party intervention. Arbitrators and mediators are often given the responsiblity for determining where the negotiations will be held. "The site for the confrontation affects the balance of situational power. If it is desirable to offset a power advantage of one party, one might do this by deliberately favoring the other in the selection of the confrontation site" (Walton, 1969, p. 8). In other words, a neutral third party can level the playing field, making the environment more conducive to joint problem solving, by selecting an appropriate bargaining site.

Notwithstanding the actual location of negotiations, formality of the setting tends to affect the bargaining behaviors of negotiators. Sommer (1965) contends that cooperatively predisposed negotiators prefer an informal, side-by-side seating arrangement, which facilitates the sharing of information and the ease of working together on common documents. Competitive negotiators, on the other hand, favor a more formal setting, where the opposing parties are seated across the table from each other. Lewicki and Litterer (1985) note that this seating arrangement allows each side to "keep an eye on the other" and to "keep the opponent at arm's length"—common colloquialisms that are often used to express the combative sentiments of each side. They conclude that "cooperative working arrangements tend to be represented by circular tables or circular arrangements of informal furniture; more competitive interactions usually occur across large, rectangular tables, with each group lined up along a side" (p. 146). The LMR model, therefore, includes:

Proposition 9: Location of negotiations affects the bargaining behaviors of grievance officials, with hosts being more cooperative than their visitors, all things equal.

Proposition 10: An informal bargaining setting fosters cooperative bargaining behavior by both grievance officials.

THE COLLECTIVE BARGAINING AGREEMENT

The collective bargaining agreement is the backbone of the parties' relationship, for it provides them with a set of principles that guides their day-to-day interactions. As with most contracts, collective bargaining agreements vary widely, from formal and

Table 6.1
Summary of Propositions on the Effects of Environmental Factors

Factor	Proposition
Economic Conditions	1. Inflation is positively related to grievance rates.
	2. Unemployment rates are inversely related to grievance rates.
	3. Management predictability of environmental conditions is inversely related to grievance rates.
Technology	4. Technology that enhances worker control over output and work variability, and that makes the job more essential to the rest of the plant, is associated with higher grievance rates.
	5. Technological change without union input is associated with higher grievance rates and less cooperative grievance behavior by union officials.
	6. Technological change that alters job content without appropriate pay and classification adjustments is associated with higher grievance rates and less cooperative grievance behavior by union officials.
Legal Regulations	7. The courts and the NLRB discourage the submission of grievances that are frivolous

highly explicit language to informal and vague understandings. Ambiguity of contract language has been identified as a main source of grievances (Slichter et al., 1960; Ross, 1963; Selby & Cunningham, 1964; Kuhn, 1967). Labig and Greer (1988, p. 14) note that "contract language that fixes only procedures of settlement without determining specific settlements often stimulate use of the grievance procedure by powerful work groups for continued bargaining during the term of the contract."

In line with these observations, Duane (1979) found high grievance rates among those community college faculty members whose bargaining agreements contained unclear step/column provisions for determining salaries. Furthermore, using the Prisoner's Dilemma game, researchers have demonstrated that cooperation is enhanced and sustained for a longer period of time when issues are clearly and distinctly presented (Evans & Crumbaugh, 1966;

Table 6.1 (Continued)

Factor	Proposition
	or devoid of merit, thereby reducing grievance rates, while promoting cooperative bargaining behavior by both grievance officials.
	8. Labor laws, along with the courts' and NLRB's interpretations of them, encourage the parties to resolve their differences jointly through the grievance process, rather than by strikes or lockouts, or other adversarial dispute-resolution mechanisms.
Bargaining Setting	9. Location of negotiations affects the bargaining behaviors of grievance officials, with hosts being more cooperative than their visitors, all things equal.
	10. An informal bargaining setting fosters cooperative bargaining behavior by both grievance officials.
Bargaining Agreement	11. Clarity of contract language is associated with low grievance rates.
	12. Clarity of contract language promotes cooperative bargaining behavior by both grievance officials.

Crumbaugh & Evans, 1967; Orwant & Orwant, 1970). Accordingly, the LMR model holds:

Proposition 11: Clarity of contract language is associated with low grievance rates.

Proposition 12: Clarity of contract language promotes cooperative bargaining behavior by both grievance officials.

CONCLUSIONS

In this chapter, several environmental factors that influence the grievance process were identified (see Table 6.1). Briefly, economic conditions affect the grievance process to the extent that inflation and a decline in the unemployment rate and in management predictability of environmental circumstances are associated with higher grievance rates. Moreover, technology generally, and advancements in technology in particular, uniquely influence the bargaining orientations of grievance officials in two ways. First, technology that grants more control to employees over their jobs and technological change that alters job content without appropriate adjustments to pay produce high grievance rates. Second, union officials tend to initiate and aggressively pursue grievances related to technological change that has occurred without their input.

It was also pointed out that the legal environment influences the parties' grievance activity. The courts and the NLRB have generally issued decisions that discourage the submission of frivolous grievances or grievances that are without merit. Moreover, recent amendments to the NLRA support the cooperative resolution of labor-management disputes.

An aspect of negotiations that is often talked about but has received limited attention from researchers is the location of negotiations. Contrary to conventional wisdom, it appears that host negotiators are more cooperative than their visitors, who are suspicious of the home-court advantage. Finally, evidence suggests that specific and clear contract language cuts down on the number of grievances and tends to facilitate the resolution of those that are filed.

7

Implications and Conclusions

At the beginning of this book, a model was introduced that highlights the role of the grievance process in labor-management cooperation. And the information presented in the succeeding chapters raised a host of important issues for future labor-management interactions. In this final chapter, some implications of the LMR model are discussed. Moreover, a framework for improving the grievance process is proposed.

IMPLICATIONS OF THE LABOR-MANAGEMENT RELATIONS MODEL

The focus of this book has been on the unidirectional effects of the various components involved in the grievance process. That is, it identified and discussed those factors that influence the grievance officials' bargaining behaviors, with added attention paid to their subsequent effects on contract negotiations, joint projects, and labor-management outcomes. Obviously, this is not the whole story. Indeed, a thorough understanding of the complex nature of union and management relations requires viewing them as having multidirectional properties (Derber, Chalmers, Edelman, &

Triandis, 1965). While the LMR model reflects this concern (see Figure 1.1) by indicating that contract negotiations and joint projects indirectly affect the grievance process (through their effects on the grievance officials' boundary-role, background, and environmental factors), a comprehensive discussion of these relationships was beyond the scope of this book. Yet, a brief recognition of them is in order.

Voos (1989) found that labor-management committees that cooperatively addressed health and safety issues tended to improve the parties' attitudes toward each other, resulting in lower grievance rates and an increased willingness to resolve grievances informally. These results are consistent with the LMR model to the extent that it posits a joint-project effect on those factors that determine bargaining orientation. In particular, when relations are improved through joint projects, as Voos suggests, boundary-role factors become more cooperatively predisposed. For example, constituents who feel better about the other side will encourage their officials to approach the grievance process more cooperatively. Furthermore, counterparts who feel better about each other will approach worker complaints differently, attempting with greater vigor to resolve them informally at first and searching for mutually satisfying solutions to those complaints that eventually are reduced to writing.

Interactions during contract negotiations also have a moderating effect on the determinants of grievance orientation. Almost by definition, cooperative contract negotiations will result in more mutually satisfying bargaining agreements, containing clearer and more specific contract language than if the parties' negotiations had been characterized by defiance and reluctant compromise. And, as noted earlier, these contractual aspects, in turn, promote cooperative grievance behavior. Moreover, the attitudinal dimensions of cooperative contract negotiations are likely to filter over into its interpretation and administration. In short, in addition to having an influence on the mode of interactions during joint projects and contract negotiations, the orientations of grievance officials are subject to feedback effects from their activities. The complexities of these interactions deserve further attention from researchers.

IMPROVING THE GRIEVANCE PROCESS

The results of this book suggest that programs oriented toward behavioral change may be effective means for improving the grievance process. Gordon and Miller (1984) investigated a number of programs that have been proposed to influence the problem-solving and conflict-resolution skills of grievance officials. For the purpose of analysis, they grouped these programs into four categories: selection, training, performance appraisal, and reward system.

Selection Programs

At the heart of selection programs is the notion that good grievance officials can be identified by reviewing their background characteristics. Gordon and Miller (1984) argue that with the exception of demonstrated leadership and problem-solving skills, little evidence exists to guide decisions with respect to the selection of grievance officials. The results of this book offer some additional wisdom in this area. First, personality profiles do not offer valuable information about how people negotiate. Instead, the research suggests that most of the personality factors presumed to drive the behavior of negotiators are under their control. Lewicki and Litterer (1985, p. 277) add that "negotiations may well be more of a 'learned' set of skills and behaviors than attributes or qualities individuals are 'born with'; hence, individuals can practice and develop these skills and behaviors to improve their effectiveness."

Second, as Gordon and Miller (1984) suggest, experienced grievance officials approach the process of resolving worker complaints differently than do novice officials. Research indicates that experienced officials are more effective negotiators primarily because they are more flexible in their bargaining styles and better equipped to face a variety of bargaining circumstances. Consistent with these attributes, said negotiators are more able to defend and fight for their parties' positions and rights when needed, but at the same time, they are open to the pursuit of cooperative solutions to problems, which does not appear to be an attribute of novice officials.

Third, the results of this book suggest that race and gender differences do not contribute significantly to variations in the bargaining orientations of grievance officials. These findings have important implications for organizational performance. Indeed selection based on these demographic attributes jeopardizes the operations and reputation of the firm, since they easily violate civil-rights laws and basic business ethics.

Training Programs

Training programs are intended to provide officials with the opportunity to gain the necessary knowledge, skills, abilities, and attitudes for effective grievance negotiations. Gordon and Miller (1984) and Bemmels et al. (1991) note that, in general, union grievance officials are better trained than their management counterparts, particularly with respect to adequate knowledge of the bargaining agreement. They recommend, therefore, that training covering contract content and administration be offered to supervisors, yet they do not provide programmatic details. In what follows, the particulars of a training program for grievance participants are presented. Much of the program is based on the principles of the mutual-gains approach (Susskind & Landry, 1991).

Session 1—*Joint training session for union members and management*. Both sides are encouraged to send any and all persons interested to a one-day training session. At this session, the trainer discusses the collective bargaining agreement, particularly the grievance procedure and those provisions that have been added or amended by recent contract negotiations. The trainer then introduces the concept of cooperative grievance negotiations, with an emphasis on an informal approach to the resolution of worker complaints. The objective here is twofold: (a) to cut down on the number of formal grievances and (b) to encourage the resolution of worker complaints between the workers and their immediate supervisors.

Session 2—*Joint training session for union and management grievance officials*. Attendance at this session is limited to union and management grievance officials. At this session, cooperative grievance negotiation is discussed in greater detail and illustrated through "*modeling*, in which trainees watch films of model persons behaving effectively in a problem situation" (Cascio, 1991, p. 382). The focus then is on active trainee participation in the form of grievance-negotiation simulations. At least some of the simulations consist of role reversals, where management officials submit *mock* grievances to their union counterparts. This session concludes with debriefing discussions, which are divided into joint reviews of simulation results and into private meetings, where each side can speak openly about their reactions to the grievance process.

Session 3—*Coaching during the life of the bargaining agreement*. When actual grievances are filed, the trainer should be available to assist both sides in searching for mutually satisfying solutions to them. It is important to note that the role of the trainer at this point is not to mediate the grievances or to offer solutions, but simply to coach the parties in cooperative grievance negotiations.

The effectiveness of grievance-negotiation training is dependent on transfer of training, which involves encouraging trainees to apply what they have learned back on the job. Trainees are likely to transfer their new knowledge and skills when they feel confident in using them; perceive them to be highly relevant to their jobs;

and, in a related matter, perceive them as ways of improving their job performance appraisals.

Performance Appraisal

The performance of union and management grievance officials is often appraised in terms of grievance activity. Conveying their reservations about this practice, Slichter et al., (1960, p. 698) comment that if "supervisors gain the impression that grievance rates will be used as a measure of managerial performance, they will see to it that the grievance statistics show the kind of results that top management desires." For some top-level managers, low grievance rates signify that the supervisors involved are performing their jobs well by addressing and resolving worker complaints before they become grievances. For other top-level managers, low rates signify that supervisors are acquiescing to too many union demands, thereby failing to carry out their responsibilities. Again, these conflicting views of what grievance activity means underscore the problem of interpreting such data without accompanying information about the circumstances that led up to their submission.

In order for any appraisal system to be used successfully, it must take a comprehensive view of performance. Clearly, grievance data, by themselves, do not explain variations in bargaining, environmental, or other relevant factors, which are likely to influence grievance rates independent of an official's negotiating skill. Accordingly, information about these factors must be taken into account when appraising the performance of officials. Moreover, grievance data do not provide feedback to the officials in terms of how they might improve their performance. They only tell them that their performance is acceptable or unacceptable. For this reason, it is recommended that descriptive performance standards be established. In addition to providing performance feedback to the official, these standards ensure consistency in supervisory judgments across individuals in the same job (Cascio, 1991). In short, grievance-data information is only one variable in a very complex performance appraisal equation.

Reward System

It is important for proper grievance-handling performance to be recognized, which entails a sound system of tangible rewards (Gordon & Miller, 1984). A study by Jennings (1974, p. 316) reveals that "foremen, while perceiving top management as regarding grievances as an important aspect of their job, neither place an extremely high priority on this activity, nor believe they are given much credit when they take initiative in resolving grievances." But, as we have seen, grievance processing should be a high-priority activity, since it profoundly affects organizational performance, including productivity, product quality, employee turnover, and strike action. Hence, there is a need for a quality reward system for grievance officials.

Regardless of their specifics, reward systems for grievance officials must comply with several conditions, including:

1. *Competitive basic pay and benefits*. To attract and retain good officials, this base must be high enough to provide a living wage without regard to isolated grievance operations or outcomes. It must also provide incentives for superior performance; incentives generally consist of 30 to 35 percent of the official's base.
2. *Impact on organizational performance*. Top-level management must recognize that effective grievance resolution really does make a difference in organizational performance. Thus, when reduced worker turnover or layoffs, enhanced productivity or product quality, or improved labor-management relations can be at least partially credited to the performance of grievance officials, they should be rewarded accordingly.

3. *Collaborate climate.* Collaboration between officials and their constituents generally, and their supervisors in particular, is mandatory. The point is that dissension and resistance only impede the performance of grievance officials.

Obviously, management has more opportunities, flexibility, and resources to satisfy these conditions than do union officials. It is recommended, therefore, that the parties work together in developing reward systems for their respective officials that encourage cooperative grievance resolution.

CONCLUDING COMMENTS

When describing the history of U.S. labor-management relations, one is hard-pressed to come up with examples where the parties have truly engaged in cooperation. But the times have changed. Competitive threats have forced unionized firms to consider alternative industrial relations systems, including labor-management cooperation. A movement toward more cooperative relations, however, will be difficult for everyone involved, but it may be the key to long-term survival and viability. In accepting this challenge, the parties must begin to restructure their relationship, and perhaps the best place to start is with the grievance process.

References

Aaron, B. (1988). The future of collective bargaining in the public sector. In B. A. Aaron, J. M. Najita, & J. L. Stern (Eds.), *Public-sector bargaining* (2nd ed.) (pp. 314–326). Washington, DC: Bureau of National Affairs.

Adams, J. S. (1963). Toward an understanding of inequity. *Journal of Abnormal and Social Psychology, 67,* 422–436.

Ahern R. W. (1982). Discussion of labor-management cooperation. *Proceedings of the Industrial Relations Research Association,* 201–206.

Anscombe, G. (1957) *Intention.* Oxford: Blackwell.

Ash, P. (1970). The parties to the grievance. *Personnel Psychology, 23,* 13–37.

AT&T Technologies, Inc. v. Communications Workers of America, 106 U.S. 1415 (1986).

Atwater, L., & Sander, S. (1984). *Quality circles in navy organizations: An evaluation.* Technical Report NPRDC TR 8453. San Diego: Navy Personnel Research Development Center.

Baron, R.A. (1971). Behavioral effects of interpersonal attraction: Compliance with requests from liked and disliked others. *Psychometric Science, 25,* 325–326.

Begin, J. P. (1971). The private grievance model in the public sector. *Industrial Relations, 10*, 21–35.

Bemmels, B., Reshef, Y., & Stratton-Devine, K. (1991). The roles of supervisors, employees, and stewards in grievance initiation. *Industrial and Labor Relations, 45*, 15–30.

Benton, A. A. (1972). Accountability and negotiations between group representatives. *Proceedings of the 80th Annual Convention of the American Psychological Association*, 227–228.

Benton, A. A., & Druckman, D. (1973). Salient solutions and the bargaining behavior of representatives and nonrepresentatives. *International Journal of Group Tensions, 3*, 28–39.

Benton, A. A., & Druckman, D. (1974). Constituent's bargaining orientation and intergroup negotiations. *Journal of Applied Social Psychology, 4*, 141–150.

Black, T. E., & Higbee, K. L. (1973). Effects of power, threat, and sex on exploitation. *Journal of Personality and Social Psychology, 27*, 382–388.

Bloom, G. F., & Northrup, H. R. (1969). *Economics in labor relations* (6th ed.). Homewood, IL: Richard D. Irwin.

Bok, D. C., & Dunlop, J. T. (1970). *Labor and the American community*. New York: Touchstone Books.

Boys Markets, Inc. v. Retail Clerks Union Local 770, 398 U.S. 235 (1970).

Braver, S. L., & Barnett, B. (1976). Effects of modeling on cooperation in a prisoner's dilemma game. *Journal of Personality and Social Psychology, 33*, 161–169.

Brett, J. M., & Goldberg, S. P. (1979). Wildcat strikes in bituminous coal mining. *Industrial and Labor Relations Review, 32*, 465–483.

Briggs, S. (1981). The grievance procedure and organizational health. *Personnel Journal, 60*, 313–319.

Bullock, R. J., & Lawler, E. E. (1984). Gainsharing: A few questions, and fewer answers. *Human Resource Management, 23*, 23–40.

Burton, J. F., & Thomason, T. (1988). The extent of collective bargaining in the public sector. In B. Aaron, J. Najita, & J. Stern (Eds.), *Public-sector bargaining* (2nd ed.), pp. 1–51. Washington, DC: Bureau of National Affairs.

Carrell, M. R., & Heavrin, C. (1991). *Collective bargaining and labor relations: Cases, practice, and law* (3rd ed.). New York: Maxwell Macmillan Press.

Cascio, W. E. (1991). *Applied psychology in personnel management* (4th ed.). Englewood Cliffs, NJ: Prentice-Hall.

Chaison, G. N., & Rose, J. B. (1991). The macrodeterminants of union growth and decline. In G. Strauss, D. Gallagher, & J. Fiorito (Eds.), *The state of the unions*. Madison, WI: IRRA.

Chamberlain, N. W. (1955). *A general theory of economic process*. New York: Harper & Row.

Chamberlain, N. W., & Kuhn, J. W. (1986). *Collective bargaining* (3rd ed.). New York: McGraw-Hill.

Chelius, J. C., & Dworkin, J. (1990). An overview of the transformation of industrial relations. In J. Chelius & J. Dworkin. *Reflections on the transformation of industrial relations*. Metuchen, NJ: Scarecrow Press.

Coke, J. S., Batson, C. D., & McDavis, K. (1978). Empathic mediation of helping: A two-stage model. *Journal of Personality and Social Psychology, 36*, 752–766.

Cole, R. E. (1980). *Work, mobility, and participation: A comparative study of American and Japanese industry*. Berkeley: University of California Press.

Conrath, D. W. (1972). Sex role and 'cooperation' in the game of chicken. *Journal of Conflict Resolution, 16*, 433–443.

Cooke, W. N. (1990). *Labor-management cooperation*. Kalamazoo, MI: W. E. Upjohn Institute for Employment Research.

Cotton, J. J., Vollrath, D. A., Froggatt, K. L., Lengnick-Hall, M. L., & Jennings, K. R. (1988). Employee participation: Diverse forms and different outcomes. *Academy of Management Review, 13*, 8–22.

Coulson, R. (1978). Fair treatment. *Arbitration journal, 33*, 23–29.

Cousineau, J., & LaCroix, R. (1986). Imperfect information and strikes: An analysis of Canadian experience, 1976–1982. *Industrial and Labor Relations Review, 39*, 539–549.

Crisci, P. E. (1986). Implementing win/win negotiating in educational institutions. *Journal of Collective Negotiations, 15* (2), 119–144.

Cross, J. G. (1969). *The economics of bargaining*. New York: Basic Books.

Crumbaugh, C. M., & Evans, G. W. (1967). Presentation format, other-person strategies, and cooperative behavior in the prisoner's dilemma. *Psychological Reports, 20*, 895–902.

Dalton, D. R., & Todor, W. D. (1985). Win, lose, draw: The grievance process in practice. *Personnel Administration, 26*, 25–29.

Dalton, D. R., & Todor, W. D. (1982). Antecedents of grievance filing behavior: Attitudes/behavioral consistency and the union steward. *Academy of Management Journal, 25*, 158–169.

Davy, J. A., Stewart, G., & Anderson, J. (1992). Formalization of grievance procedures: A multi-firm and industry study. *Journal of Labor Research, 13*, 307–316.

Dean, L. R. (1954). Union activity and dual loyalty. *Industrial and Labor Relations Review, 7*, 519–530.

Derber, M., Chalmers, W. E., Edelman, M. T., & Triandis, H. C. (1965). *Plant union-management relations: From practice to theory*. Urbana: University of Illinois.

Diaz, E. M., Minton, J. W., & Saunders, D. M. (1987). A fair nonunion grievance procedure. *Personnel, 39*, 13–27.

Druckman, D. (1967). Dogmatism, prenegotiation experience, and simulated group representation as determinants of dyadic behavior in a bargaining situation. *Journal of Personality and Social Psychology, 6*, 279–290.

Druckman, D., Solomon, D., & Zechmeister, K. (1972). Effects of representational role obligations on the process of children's distribution of resources. *Sociometry, 35*, 387–410.

Duane, M. J. (1979). Faculty grievances: An aid to the college administrator. *Journal of Collective Negotiations in the Public Sector, 8*, 279–290.

Duane, M. J. (1984). The determinants of bargaining orientation for first-level grievance representatives at secondary buildings in Minnesota. Unpublished doctoral dissertation, University of Minnesota.

Duane, M. J. (1989). Sex differences in styles of conflict management. *Psychological Reports, 65*, 1033–1034.

Duane, M. J. (1990). Determinants of bargaining behavior in grievance negotiations. Unpublished manuscript, University of Minnesota, Industrial Relations Center, Minneapolis.

Duane, M. J. (1991a). Applying equity theory to compensation. In J. Jones, B. Steffy, & D. Bray (Eds.), *Applying psychology in business: The handbook for managers and human resource professionals* (pp. 384–389). Lexington, MA: Lexington Books.

Duane, M. J. (1991b). To grieve or not grieve: Why 'reduce it to writing?' *Public Personnel Management*, *20*, 83–90.

Duane, M. J., Azevedo, R. E., & Anderson, U. (1985). Behavior as an indication of an opponent's intentions in collective negotiations. *Psychological Reports*, *57*, 507–513.

Duane, M. J., Azevedo, R. E., & Rhee Y. S. (1987). Location of Negotiations: My place or yours? *Journal of Collective Negotiations in the Public Sector*, *16*, 377–383.

Duval, S., & Duval, V. H. (1983). *Consistency and cognition: A theory of causal attribution*. Hillside, NJ: Erbaum.

Eaton, A. E., Gordon, M. E., & Keefe, J. H. (1992). The impact of quality of work life programs and grievance system effectiveness on union commitment. *Industrial and Labor Relations Review*, *45*, 591–604.

Eckerman, A. C. (1948). An analysis of grievances and aggrieved employees in a machine shop and foundry. *Journal of Applied Psychology*, *32*, 255–269.

Evans, G. W., & Crumbaugh, C. M. (1966). Effects of prisoner's dilemma format on cooperative behavior. *Journal of Personality and Social Psychology*, *5*, 87–88.

Feuille, P., & Wheeler, H. N. (1981). Will the real industrial conflict please stand up? In J. Stieber, R. B. McKersie, & D. Q. Mills (Eds.), *U.S. industrial relations 1950–1980: A critical assessment*. Madison, WI: Industrial Relations Research Association, 255–295.

Fisher, R. (1964). Fractionating conflict. In R. Fisher (Ed.), *International conflict and behavioral science: The Craigville papers*. New York: Basic Books.

Fisher, R., & Ury, W. (1981). *Getting to yes: Negotiating agreements without giving in*. Boston: Houghton Mifflin.

Fleishman, E. A., & Harris, E. F. (1962). Patterns of leadership behavior related to employee grievances and turnover. *Personnel Psychology*, *15*, 43–56.

Fleming, R. W., & Witte, E. E. (1959). Grievances under the collective agreement. In J. Barbash (Ed.), *Unions and union leadership*. New York: Harper.

Fossum, J. A. (1989). *Labor Relations* (4th ed.). Homewood, IL: BPI/Irwin.

Franklin, S. (1992, April 15). At Caterpillar's gates both sides claim victory. *Chicago Tribune*, p. 14.

Freedman, A. (1979). *Managing labor relations*. New York: Conference Board.

Freedman, A. (1985). *The new look in wage bargaining*. New York: Conference Board.

Freeman, R. B., & Medoff, J. (1984). *What do unions do?* New York: Basic Books.

Fry, W. R., Firestone, I. J., & William, D. (1979). Bargaining process in mixed-singles dyads: Loving and losing. *Proceedings of the Eastern Psychological Association.*

Gandz, J. (1979). Grievance initiation and resolution: A test of the behavioural theory. *Relations Industrielles*, *34*, 778–792.

Gandz, J., & Whitehead, J. D. (1981). The relationship between industrial relations climate and grievance initiation and resolution. *Proceedings of the Industrial Relations Research Association*, 778–791.

Garcia v. San Antonio Metropolitan Transit Authority, 105 U.S. 1005 (1985).

Geare, A. J. (1976). Productivity from Scanlon-type plans. *Academy of Management Review*, *1*, 99–108.

Glassman, A. M., & Belasco, J. A. (1975). The chapter chairman and school grievances. *Industrial Relations*, *14*, 233–241.

Gordon, M. E., & Miller, S. J. (1984). Grievances: A review of research and practice. *Personnel Psychology*, *37*, 117–146.

Graham, H., & Heshizer, B. (1979). The effect of contract language on low-level settlement of grievances. *Labor Law Journal*, *30*, 427–432.

Grant, M., & Sermat, V. (1969). Status and sex of other as determinants of behavior in a mixed-motive game. *Journal of Personality and Social Psychology*, *12*, 151–157.

Green, B. F., & Hall, J. A. (1984). Quantitative methods for literature reviews. *Annual Review of Psychology*, *35*, 37–53.

Griffin, R. W. (1988). Consequences of quality circles in an industrial setting: A longitudinal assessment. *Academy of Management Journal*, *31*, 338–358.

Gruder, C. L. (1971). Relationship with opponent and partner in mixed-motive bargaining. *Journal of Conflict Resolution*, *15*, 403–416.

Gryna, F. M. (1981). *Quality circles: A team approach to problem solving*. New York: AMACOM.

Guzzo, R. A., Jette, R. D., & Katzell, R. A. (1985). The effects of psychologically based intervention programs on work productivity: A meta-analysis. *Personnel Psychology*, *38*, 275–291.

Hammer, T. H. (1988). New developments in profit sharing, gainsharing, and employee ownership. In J. P. Campbell, R. J. Campbell, & Associates (Eds.), *Productivity in organizations*. San Francisco: Jossey-Bass.

Harnett, D. L., Cummings, W. S., & Hamner, W. C. (1973). Personality, bargaining style, and payoff in bilateral monopoly bargaining among European managers. *Sociometry*, *36*, 325–345.

Harnett, D. L., Cummings, W. S., & Hughes, G. D. (1968). The influence of risk-taking propensity on bargaining behavior. *Behavioral Science*, *13*, 91–101.

Havlovic, S. J. (1991). Quality of work life and human resource outcomes. *Industrial Relations*, *30* (3), 469–479

Heneman, H. G., Schwab, D. P., Fossum, J. A., & Dyer, L. D. (1989). *Personnel/human resource management* (4th ed.). Homewood, IL: Richard D. Irwin.

Hirsch, B. T. (1992). Firm investment behavior and collective bargaining strategy. *Industrial Relations*, *31* (1), 95–121.

Holley, W., & Jennings, K. (1988). *The labor relations process* (3rd ed.). Chicago: Dryden Press.

Hornstein, H. A. (1976). *Cruelty and kindness: A new look at aggression and altruism*. Englewood Cliffs, NJ: Prentice-Hall.

Ichniowski, C. (1986). The effects of grievance activity on productivity. *Industrial and Labor Relations Review*, *40* (1), 75–89.

Ichniowski, C., & Lewin, D. (1987). Grievance procedures and firm performance. In M. Kleiner, R. Block, M. Roomkin, & S. Salsburg (Eds.), *Human resources and the performance of the firm* (pp. 159–193). Madison, WI: Industrial Relations Research Association Series.

Ingle, S., & Ingle, N. (1983). *Quality circles in service industries: Comprehensive guidelines for increased productivity and efficiency*. Englewood Cliffs, NJ: Prentice-Hall.

Jennings, K. (1974). Foremen's views of their involvement with the union steward in the grievance process. *Labor Law Journal*, *25*, 305–316.

Kaplan, A. (1950). *Making grievance procedures work.* Los Angeles: University of California Press.

Katz, H. C., & Kochan, T. A. (1992). *An introduction to collective bargaining and industrial relations.* New York: McGraw-Hill, Inc.

Katz, H. C., Kochan, T. A., & Gobeille, K. R. (1983). Industrial relations performance, economic performance, and QWL programs: An interplant analysis. *Industrial and Labor Relations Review, 37* (1), 3–17.

Katz, H. C., Kochan, T. A., & Weber, M. (1985). Assessing the effects of industrial relations systems and quality of working life efforts on organizational effectiveness. *Academy of Management Journal, 28,* 509–526.

Kaufman, B. E. (1986). *The economics of labor markets and labor relations.* Chicago: Dryden Press.

Kelley, M. R., & Harrison, B. (1991). Unions, technology, and labor-management cooperation. In L. Mishel & P. B. Voos (Eds.), *Unions and Economic Competitiveness.* New York: M. E. Sharpe.

Kennedy, T. (1980). *European labor relations.* Lexington, MA: Lexington Books.

Keys, J. B., & Miller, T. R. (1984). The Japanese management theory jungle. *Academy of Management Review, 9,* 342–353.

Kleiner, M. M., Nickelsburg, G., & Pilarski, A. M. (1988). Grievances and plant performance is zero optimal? In B. D. Dennis (Ed.), *Proceedings of the Forty-First Annual Meeting of the Industrial Relations Research Association Series.* Madison, WI, 172–180.

Kleiner, M. M., Nickelsburg, G., & Pilarski, A. M. (1991). Monitoring, grievances, and plant performance. Unpublished manuscript. University of Minnesota.

Klimoski, R. J., & Ash, R. A. (1974). Accountability and negotiation behavior. *Organizational Behavior and Human Performance, 11,* 409–425.

Kochan, T. A. (1980). *Collective bargaining and industrial relations.* Homewood, IL: Richard D. Irwin.

Kochan, T. A., Katz, H. C., & McKersie, R. B. (1986). *The transformation of American industrial relations.* New York: Basic Books.

Kochan, T. A., McKersie, R. B., & Chalykoff, J. (1986). The effects of corporate strategy and workplace innovation on union representation. *Industrial and Labor Relations Review, 39* (4), 487–501.

Komorita, S. S., & Esser, J. K. (1975). Frequency of reciprocated concessions in bargaining. *Journal of Personality and Social Psychology, 32*, 699–705.

Konowe, J. (1983). Union official addresses impact of "robotic revolution" on workers. *Daily Labor Report*, April issue.

Kuhn, J. W. (1961). *Bargaining in grievance settlement: The power of industrial work group*. New York: Columbia Press.

Kuhn, J. W. (1967). Bargaining in grievance settlements. In J. T. Dunlop & N. W. Chamberlain (Eds.), *Frontiers of collective bargaining* (pp. 252–270). New York: Harper and Row.

Kuhns, R. (1986). Win/win negotiating—process or philosophy. *Journal of Collective Negotiations, 15* (3), 281–287.

Labig, C. E., & Greer, C. R. (1988). Grievance initiation: A literature survey and suggestions for future research. *Journal of Labor Research, 9*, 1–27.

Lawler, E. E. (1986). *High-involvement management: Participative strategies for improving organizational performance*. San Francisco: Jossey-Bass.

Ledford, G. E., Lawler, E. E., & Mohrman, S. A. (1988). The quality circle and its variations. In J. P. Campbell, R. J. Campbell, & Associates (Eds.), *Productivity in organizations* (pp. 255–294). San Francisco: Jossey-Bass.

Leone, R. C. (1982). *The operation of area labor-management committees*. Washington, DC: U.S. Department of Labor, Labor-Management Services Administration.

Levinson, H. (1980). Trucking. In G. G. Somers (Ed.), *Collective bargaining: Contemporary American experience* (pp. 128–129). Madison, WI: Industrial Relations Research Association.

Lewicki, R. J., & Litterer, J. A. (1985). *Negotiation*. Homewood, IL: Richard D. Irwin.

MacDonald, R. M. (1967). Collective bargaining in the postwar period. *Industrial and Labor Relations Review, 20*, 553–577.

Macy, B., & Peterson, M. (1981). Evaluating attitudinal change in a longitudinal quality of work life intervention. Paper presented at the annual meeting of the Academy of Management, San Diego.

Marks, M. L., Mirvis, P. H., Hackett, E. J., & Grady, J. F. (1986). Employee participation in a quality circle program: Impact on quality of work life, productivity, and absenteeism. *Journal of Applied Psychology*, *71*, 61–68.

Marshall, F. R., & Briggs, V. M. (1989). *Labor economics: Theory, institutions, public policy* (6th ed.). Homewood, IL: Richard D. Irwin.

Martindale, D. A. (1971). Territorial dominance behavior in dyadic verbal interactions. *Proceedings of the 79th Annual Convention of the American Psychological Association*, *6*, 305–306.

McKersie, R. B. (1964). Avoiding written grievances by problem-solving: An outside view. *Personnel Psychology*, *17*, 367–379.

McKersie, R. B., & Shropshire, W. S. (1965). Avoiding written grievances: A successful program. *The Chicago Journal of Business*, *35*, 135–152.

McNeel, S. P., McClintock, C. G., & Nuttin, J. M. (1972). Effects of sex role in a two-person mixed-motive game. *Journal of Personality and Social Psychology*, *24*, 372–349.

Milkovich, G., & Newman, J. (1990). *Compensation* (3rd ed.). Homewood, IL: Richard D. Irwin.

Miller, G. H., & Pyke, S. W. (1973). Sex, matrix variations, and perceived personality effects in mixed-motive games. *Journal of Conflict Resolution*, *17*, 335–349.

Mills, D. Q. (1980). Construction. In G. G. Somers (Ed.), *Collective bargaining: Contemporary American experience* (pp. 86–89). Madison, WI: Industrial Relations Research Association.

Mills, D. Q. (1989). *Labor-management relations* (4th ed.). New York: McGraw-Hill.

Mitchell, D. (1982). Recent union contract concession. *Brookings Pagers on Economic Activity*, *1*, 165–204.

Mohrman, S. A., & Novelli, L. (1985). Beyond testimonials: Learning from a quality circle programme. *Journal of Occupational Behavior*, *6*, 93–110.

Mullen, J. H. (1954). The supervisor assesses his job in management. *Personnel*, *31*, 94–108.

Mullick, B., & Lewis, S. A. (1977). Sex-roles, loving and liking: A look at dating couples' bargaining. *Proceedings of the 85th Annual Convention of the American Psychological Association.*

Munchus, G. (1983). Employer-employee based quality circles in Japan: Human resource policy implications for American firms. *Academy of Management Review*, *8*, 255–261.

National Labor Relations Board, Office of the General Counsel. *Memorandum* 79-55, July 9, 1979.

National League of Cities v. Usery, 426 U.S. 833 (1976).

Nisbett, R. E., & Schachter, S. (1966). Cognitive manipulation of pain. *Journal of Experimental Social Psychology, 2*, 227–236.

Norsworthy, J. R., & Zabala, C. A. (1985). Worker attitudes, worker behavior, and productivity in the U.S. automobile industry, 1959–1979. *Industrial and Labor Relations Review, 38*, 544–557.

Nurick, A. J. (1982). Participation in organizational change: A longitudinal field study. *Human Relations, 35*, 413–430.

Organ, D. W. (1971). Some variables affecting boundary role behavior. *Sociometry, 34*, 524–537.

Orwant, C. J., & Orwant, J. E. (1970). A comparison of interpreted and abstract versions of mixed-motive games. *Journal of Conflict Resolution, 14*, 91–97.

Peach, D. A., & Livernash, E. R. (1974). *Grievance initiation and resolution: A study in basic steel*. Boston: Harvard University Press.

Pen, J. (1952). A general theory of bargaining. *American Economic Review, 42*, 24–42.

Peterson, R. B. (1990). Thoughts on the transformation of industrial relations. In J. Chelius & J. Dworkin (Eds.), *Reflections on the transformation of industrial relations*. Metuchen, NJ: Scarecrow Press.

Peterson, R. B., & Lewin, D. (1981). A model for research and analysis of the grievance process. *Proceedings of the Industrial Relations Research Association*, 303–312.

Pfeffer, J. (1982). *Organizations and organization theory*. Boston: Pitman.

Piore, M. (1991). The future of unions. In G. Strauss, D. Gallagher, & J. Fiorito (Eds.), *The state of the unions* (pp. 378–426). Madison, WI: IRRA.

Price, J., DeWire, J., Nowack, J., Schenkel, K., & Ronan, W. (1976). Three studies of grievances. *Personnel Journal*, 33–37.

Pruitt, D. G. (1968). Reciprocity and credit building in dyads. *Journal of Personality and Social Psychology, 8*, 143–147.

Pruitt, D. G. (1981). *Negotiation behavior*. New York: Academic Press.

Purcell, T. V. (1953). *The worker speaks his mind*. Boston: Harvard University Press.

Rees, A. (1952). Industrial conflict and business fluctuations: *Journal of Political Economy, 60*, 371–382.

Rees, D. I. (1991). Grievance procedure strength and teacher quits. *Industrial and Labor Relations Review, 45*, 31–43.

Reynolds, L. G., Masters, S. H., & Moser, C. H. (1986). *Labor economics and labor relations* (9th ed.). Englewood Cliffs, NJ: Prentice-Hall.

Rosnow, R. L., & Rosenthal, R. (1989). Statistical procedures and the justification of knowledge in psychological science. *American Psychologist, 44*, 1276–1284.

Ross, A. M. (1963). Distressed grievance procedures and their rehabilitation. In M. L. Kahn (Ed.), *Labor arbitration and industrial change* (pp. 104–132). Washington, DC: Bureau of National Affairs.

Rubin, J. A., & Brown, B. R. (1975). *The social psychology of bargaining negotiation*. New York: Academic Press.

Sauer, R. L., & Voelker, K. E. (1993). *Labor relations: Structure and process* (2nd ed.). New York: Macmillan.

Schachter, H. L. (1989). Win-win bargaining: A new spirit in school negotiations? *Journal of Collective Negotiations, 18 (1)*, 1–8.

Schlossberg, S. I., & Fetter, S. M. (1986). *U.S. labor law and the future of labor-management cooperation*. Washington, DC: U.S. Department of Labor.

Schuster, M. H. (1983). The impact of union-management cooperation on productivity and employment. *Industrial and Labor Relations Review, 36*, 415–430.

Schuster, M. H. (1984a). The Scanlon plan: A longitudinal analysis. *Journal of Applied Behavioral Science, 20*, 23–28.

Schuster, M. H. (1984b). *Union-Management cooperation*. Kalamazoo, MI: Upjohn Institute.

Selby, R. T., & Cunningham, M. T. (1964). Grievance procedures in major contracts. *Monthly Labor Review, 87*, 1125–1130.

Serrin, W. (1973). *The company and the union*. New York: Alfred A. Knopf.

Sherman, A. W., & Bohlander, G. W. (1992). *Managing human resources (9th ed.)*. Cincinnati: South-Western Publishing Co.

Sinclair Refining Co. v. Atkinson, 370 U.S. 195 (1962).

Singerman, K. J., Barkovec, T. D., & Baron, R. S. (1976). Failure of a misattribution therapy manipulation with a clinically relevant target behavior. *Behavior Therapy, 7*, 306–316.

Slichter, S. H., Healy, J. J., & Livernash, E. R. (1960). *The impact of collective bargaining on management.* Washington, DC: The Brookings Institution.

Sloane, A. A., & Whitney, F. (1981). *Labor relations* (4th ed.). Englewood Cliffs, NJ: Prentice-Hall.

Sommer, R. (1965). Further studies of small group ecology. *Sociometry, 28*, 337–348.

Spencer, D. (1986). Employee voice and employee retention. *Academy of Management Journal, 29*, 488–502.

Staub, E. (1978). *Positive social behavior and morality (Vol. 1): Social and personal influences.* New York: Academic Press.

Steel, R. P., & Shane, G. S. (1986). Evaluation research on quality circles: Technical and analytical implications. *Human Relations, 39*, 449–468.

Sulkin, H. A., & Pranis, R. W. (1967). Comparison of grievants with non-grievants in a heavy machinery company. *Personnel Psychology, 20*, 111–119.

Susskind, L. E., & Landry, E. M. (1991). Implementing a mutual gains approach to collective bargaining. *Negotiations Journal*, January.

Taylor, B. J., & Witney, F. (1987). *Labor relations law* (5th ed.). Englewood Cliffs, NJ: Prentice-Hall.

Textile Workers Union v. Lincoln Mills, 355 U.S. 448 (1957).

Thomas, R. (1991). Technological choice and union-management cooperation. *Industrial Relations, 30*, 167–192.

Thomas, S. (1989). Two-tier collective bargaining agreements and firm performance. In J. Burton (Ed.). *Proceedings of the Forty-second Annual Meeting of the Industrial Relations Research Association Series*, December, 150–162.

Thomson, A. J., & Murray, V. V. (1976). *Grievance procedures.* Westmead, England: Saxon House.

United Paperworkers International Union, AFL-CIO v. Misco, Inc., 108 U.S. 364 (1987).

United States Department of Labor. (1990). *The new work systems network.* (BLMR 136). Washington, DC: U.S. Government Printing Office.

United Steelworkers of America, Local Union 2610 (Bethlehem Steel), 255 NLRB 54 (1976).

United Steelworkers of America v. American Manufacturing Co., 363 U.S. 564 (1960).

United Steelworkers of America v. Enterprise Wheel and Car Corp., 363 U.S. 593 (1960).

United Steelworkers of America v. Warrior & Gulf Navigation Co., 363 U.S. 574 (1960).

Verma, A., & McKersie, R. B. (1987). Employee involvement: the implications of noninvolvement by unions. *Industrial and Labor Relations Review*, *15*, 556–568.

Voos, P. B. (1989). The influence of cooperation program on union-management relations, flexibility, and other labor relations outcomes. *Journal of Labor Research*, *10* (1), 105–117.

Wagar, T. H., & Robinson, J. F. (1989). Determinants of grievance outcomes in a nonunion setting: Some evidence from Virginia. *Proceedings of the 42nd Annual Meeting*, December, 567.

Wall, J. A., & Adams, J. S. (1974). Some variables affecting a constituent's evaluations of and behavior toward a boundary role occupant. *Organizational Behavior and Human Performance*, *11*, 390–408.

Wall Street Journal. June 5, 1970.

Walton, R. E. (1969). *Interpersonal peacekeeping: Confrontations and third-party consultation*. Reading, MA: Addison-Wesley.

Walton, R. E., & McKersie, R. B. (1965). *A behavioral theory of labor negotiations*. New York: McGraw-Hill.

Werther, W. B., Ruch, W. A., & McClure, L. (1986). *Productivity through people*. St. Paul: West Publishing Co.

Whyte, W. (1967). Patterns for interactions in union management relations. In W. Faunce (Ed.), *Reading in industrial sociology*. New York: Appleton-Century-Crofts.

Work in American Institute, Inc. (1982). *Productivity through work innovation*. New York: Pergamon Press.

Wyer, R. S., & Malinowski, C. (1972). Effects of sex and achievement level upon individualism and competitiveness in social interaction. *Journal of Experimental Social Psychology*, *8*, 303–314.

Name Index

Aaron, B., 70
Adams, J. S., 79, 96
Ahern, R. W., 30
Anderson, J., 84
Anderson, U., 104
Anscombe, G., 104
Ash, P., 82, 92, 94
Ash, R. A., 97
Atwater, L., 29
Azevedo, R., 104, 121

Barkovec, T. D., 104
Barnett, B., 105
Baron, R. S., 103, 105
Batson, C. D., 103
Begin, J. P., 82, 98–99
Belasco, J. A., 97
Bemmels, B., 93, 99, 130
Benton, A. A., 97
Black, T. E., 93
Bloom, G. F., 85
Bohlander, G. W., 15, 18
Bok, D. C., 4
Braver, S. L., 105
Brett, J. M., 78
Briggs, S., 30, 82
Briggs, V. M., 3
Brown, B. R., 90, 121
Bullock, R. J., 14, 21
Burton, J. F., 37, 70

Carrell, M. R., 39, 50–51
Cascio, W. E., 21, 25, 32, 131–32
Chaison, G. N., 39
Chalmers, W. E., 127
Chalykoff, J., 4
Chamberlain, N. W., 2–3, 6, 8, 32, 55, 57, 64, 68–69, 110
Chelius, J. C., 1, 38
Coke, J. S., 103
Cole, R. E., 25

Conrath, D. W., 93
Cooke, W. N., 4–5, 8, 24, 29, 31, 38, 40, 46
Cotton, J. J., 31
Coulson, R., 71
Cousineau, J., 110
Crisci, P. E., 8
Cross, J. G., 8
Crumbaugh, C. M., 124–25
Cunningham, M. T., 124

Dalton D. R., 74, 98
Davy, J. A., 84, 91
Dean, L. R., 101
Derber, M., 126
DeWire, J., 94
Diaz, E. M., 71
Douglas, William O., 117–18
Druckman, D., 90, 96–97
Duane, M. J., 30, 51, 59, 64, 66, 74, 84–85, 91–93, 97–98, 103–5, 122, 124
Dunlop, J. T., 4
Duval, S., 104
Duval, V. H., 104
Dworkin, J., 1, 38
Dyer, L. D., 15

Eaton, A. E., 31, 81
Eckerman, A. C., 94, 95
Edelman, M. T., 127
Esser, J. K., 104
Evans, G. W., 124–25

Fetter, S. M., 120
Feuille, P., 83
Firestone, I. J., 102
Fisher, R., 52–53, 55–56, 122
Fleishman, E. A., 100
Fleming, R. W., 101
Fossum, J. A., 15, 25–27, 30, 48, 67, 72, 83, 119
Franklin, S., 42
Freedman, A., 40
Freeman, R. B., 8, 61, 75, 78
Froggatt, K. L., 31
Fry, W. R., 103

Gandz, J., 82, 101
Geare, A. J., 31, 193
Glassman, A. M., 98
Gobeille, K. R., 8
Goldberg, S. P., 78
Gompers, Samuel, 35
Gordon, M. E., 31, 84, 129–30, 133
Grady, J. F., 29
Graham, H., 85
Grant, M., 93
Green, B. F., 21
Green, William, 1
Greer, C. R., 81, 83, 92, 94, 99, 101, 111, 124
Griffin, R. W., 25
Gruder, C. L., 97, 104
Gryna, F. M., 25
Guzzo, R. A., 21

Hackett, E. J., 29
Hall, J. A., 21
Hammer, T. H., 14–15, 20, 22
Harnett, D. L., 90
Harris, E. F., 100
Harrison, B., 30
Havlovic, S. J., 8, 29
Healy, J. J., 30
Heavrin, C., 39, 50–51
Heneman, H. G., 15

Heshizer, B., 85
Higbee, K. L., 93
Hirsch, B. T., 54
Holley, W., 50, 64, 66–67
Hornstein, H. A., 103

Ichniowski, C., 8, 64, 75–78, 85
Ingle, N., 25
Ingle, S., 25

Jennings, K. R., 31, 50, 64, 66–67, 112, 133
Jette, R. D., 21

Kaplan, A., 101
Katz, H. C., 1, 8, 32, 36, 38, 40, 43–46, 49, 74, 78
Katzell, R. A., 21
Kaufman, B. E., 110
Keefe, J. H., 31
Kelley, M. R., 30
Kennedy, John F., 36–37
Kennedy, T., 72–73
Keys, J. B., 25
Kleiner, M. M., 80
Klimoski, R. J., 97
Kochan, T. A., 1, 4, 8, 32, 36, 38, 40, 43–46, 49, 74, 109
Komorita, S. S., 104
Konowe, Joseph, 112
Kuhn, J. W., 3, 6, 8, 32, 55, 57, 59, 64–65, 110–11
Kuhns, R., 8

Labig, C. E., 81, 83, 92, 94, 99, 101, 111, 124
LaCroix, R., 110
Landry, E. M., 57, 130
Lawler, E. E., 14–15, 21
Ledford, G. E., 25, 33
Lengnick-Hall, M., 31
Leone, R. C., 27
Levinson, H., 69
Lewicki, R. J., 53, 55, 90–91, 121, 123, 129
Lewin, D., 64, 75–78, 82, 85
Lewis, S. A., 102
Litterer, J. A., 53, 55, 90–91, 121, 123, 129
Livernash, E. R., 30, 82–83, 99, 101, 111

MacDonald, R. M., 36
Macy, B., 31
Malinowski, C., 93
Marks, M. L., 29
Marshall, F. R., 3
Martindale, D. A., 121
Masters, S. H., 2
McClintock, C. G., 93
McClure, L., 17, 19, 23
McDavis, K., 103
McKersie, R. B., 1, 4, 13, 25, 30, 32, 36, 38, 40, 43–46, 49, 52, 82, 99
McNeel, S. P., 93
Medoff, J., 8, 61, 75
Milkovich, G., 51
Miller, G. H., 93
Miller, S. J., 31, 84, 129–30
Miller, T. R., 25
Mills, D. Q., 54, 69
Minton, J. W., 71
Mirvis, P. H., 29
Mitchell, D., 36
Mohrman, S. A., 25, 29
Mondale, Walter, 37
Moser, C. H., 2

Mullen, J. H., 84
Mullick, B., 103
Munchus, G., 25
Murray, V., 64

Newman, J., 51
Nickelsburg, G., 80
Nisbett, R. E., 104
Norsworthy, J. R., 78
Northrup, H. R., 85
Novelli, L., 29
Nowack, J., 94
Nurick, A. J., 31
Nuttin, J. M., 93

Organ, D. W., 97
Orwant, C. J., 125
Orwant, J. E., 125

Peach, D. A., 82–83, 99, 101, 111
Pen, J., 2
Peterson, M., 31, 36, 82
Pfeffer, J., 96
Pilarski, A., 80
Piore, J., 37
Pranis, R. W., 94
Price, J., 94
Pruitt, D. G., 93, 97, 103–4
Purcell, T. V., 92
Pyke, S. W., 93

Rees, A., 110
Rees, D.I., 75
Reshef, Y., 93
Reynolds, L. G., 2, 77
Rhee, Y., 121
Rich, Marc, 47–48
Robinson, J. F., 93
Ronan, W., 94
Rose, J. B., 39
Rosenthal, R., 21
Rosnow, R. L., 21
Ross, A. M., 124
Rubin, J. A., 90, 121
Ruch, W. A., 17, 19, 23

Sander, S., 29
Sauer, R. L., 72–74
Saunders, D. M., 71
Schachter, H. L., 8, 53
Schachter, S., 104
Schenkel, K., 94
Schlossberg, S. I., 120
Schuster, M. H., 8, 16–18, 20–22
Schwab, D. P., 15
Selby, R. T., 124
Sermat, V., 93
Serrin, W., 74
Shane, G. S., 28
Sherman, A. W., 15, 18
Shropshire, W. S., 99
Singerman, K. J., 104
Slichter, S. H., 30, 79, 82–85, 99, 101–2, 112, 124, 132
Sloane, A. A., 82
Solomon, D., 97
Sommer, R., 123
Spencer, D., 76
Staub, E., 103
Steel, R. P., 28
Stewart, G., 84
Strasser, Adolph, 35
Stratton-Devine, K., 93
Suklin, H. A., 94
Susskind, L. E., 57, 130

Taylor, B. J., 114–15

Thomas, R., 112
Thomas, S., 51
Thomason, T., 37, 70
Thomson, A. J., 64
Todor, W. D., 74, 98
Triandis, H. C., 128

Ury, W., 52–53, 55–56, 122

Verma, A., 13, 25, 30
Voelker, K. E., 72–74
Vollrath, D. A., 31
Voos, P. B., 8, 128

Wagar, T. H., 93
Wall, J. A., 96
Walton, R. E., 52, 122
Weber, M., 78
Werther, W. B., 17, 19, 23
Wheeler, H. E., 83
Whitehead, J. D., 82
Whitney, 82
Whyte, W., 101
Williams, D., 103
Witney, F., 114–15, 119
Witte, E. E., 101
Wyer, R. S., 93

Zabala, C. A., 78
Zechmeister, K., 97

Subject Index

Allied Industrial Workers of America Union, 50
Amalgamated Clothing and Textile Workers Union, 47, 57
American Airlines, 44, 51
Anti-union activities. *See* Union avoidance
Arbitration, 64–67, 69, 73–77, 85, 91, 116–19
Area-Wide Labor Management Committees (AWLMC). *See* Labor-management programs
AT&T Technologies, Inc. v. Communications Workers of America, 119

Bargaining power, 1–4, 8, 49
Bituminous Coal Operators Association, 57
Boulwarism, 36
Boundary-role factors, 10–12, 89, 95–108, 128; constituent demands, 96–102; officials' relationship, 103–8
Boys Markets, Inc. v. Retail Clerks, 119
Briggs & Stratton Company, 50

Caterpillar Tractor Company, 41, 45, 48, 50, 121
Chrysler Corporation, 48, 51, 56
Contract negotiations, 2, 11, 35–61, 63, 81, 85, 100, 127–28, 130; adversarial, 10, 82; at American Airlines, 44; cooperative, 8, 10, 35, 52–60, 82; training and, 57–59
Corporate campaign, 46–48
Czechoslovakia, 47

Decertification election, 39–40, 61
Double-breasted firms, 38–39

Eastern Airlines, 48
Employee Stock Ownership Program (ESOP), 47–48
Environmental factors, 8, 9–11, 109–26, 128; bargaining setting, 121–23; collective bargaining agreement, 123–25; economic conditions, 109–11; legal regulations, 114–21; technology, 111–14
Executive Order 10988, 37
Executive Order 11616, 69

Fair Labor Standards Act, 70
Federal Mediation and Conciliation Service (FMCS), 67
Florida East Coast Railway, 45

Garcia v. San Antonio Metropolitan Transit Authority, 70
General Motors Corporation, 43, 54, 74
Giant Foods Company, 50
Grievance procedures, 63–67; agriculture, construction, and trucking, 68–69; employee turnover and, 75–77; international, 72–74; nonunion, 70–72; productivity and, 78–80; public sector, 69–70; strikes and, 77–78
Grievance rates: analysis of, 66, 82–84; bargaining agreement and, 124–25; contract negotiations and, 81–82, 86; economic conditions and, 110; grievance official training and, 93; legal regulations and, 116; management policies and, 100–102; performance appraisal and, 132; productivity and, 78–80, 86; technology and, 111, 114; union policies and, 98–100

Improshare program. *See* Labor-management programs
Inducement-to-agree ratio, 2–3
Ingalls Shipbuilding Company, 50
International Harvester Company, 99

J. P. Stevens Company, 47

Labor-management Cooperation Act, 27–28
Labor-management cooperation, 52–62; controlling issues and, 53–55; integrative frameworks and, 55–60
Labor-management programs: Area-Wide Labor Management Committees, 26–30; benefits of, 4–7, 13, 18, 60; costs of, 5–6, 29, 33; gainsharing, 23–30; Improshare, 20–23; nongainsharing, 32–39; Quality circles, 23–26, 28–29; Rucker, 18–20, 22; Scanlon, 16–18, 23; union versus nonunion, 13, 25, 30
Lockouts, 2–3, 42, 72, 121, 125

Meta-analysis, 21
Modern Operating Agreement (MOA), 56–57
Mutual-gains approach: contract negotiations, 57–59; grievance negotiations, 130–32

National Labor Relations Act (NLRA), 6, 36, 45, 70, 114, 116, 120
National Labor Relations Board (NLRB), 36, 39, 45, 114, 116, 120–21
National League of Cities v. Usery, 70
National Public Employee Relations Committee, 70
National Steel Corporation, 48
Negotiating skill, 3, 58, 60, 91–92, 129–32
Norris-LaGuardia Act, 118
North American Aviation Company, 114

Organizing campaigns, 37, 39, 41, 61

Packard Electric Company, 50
Pan American Airlines, 48
Pattern bargaining, 40–42
Phelps Dodge Company, 45
Productivity: collective bargaining and, 56–57; gainsharing and, 14–16, 18, 20, 21; grievance process and, 63, 75, 78–80, 85–86, 133; nongainsharing and, 23–24, 26, 29; labor-management programs and, 5–7, 31; technology and, 111; two-tier wage programs and, 51; union-avoidance and, 61; working-to-rules policy and, 48

Quality circles. *See* Labor-management programs

Rath Packing Company, 48
Ravenswood Aluminum Corporation, 45, 47–48
Romania, 47
Rucker program. *See* Labor-management programs
Russia, 47

Scanlon program. *See* Labor-management programs
Senate Education and Labor Committee, 1
Sinclair Refining Co. v. Atkinson, 118
Skill-based pay, 57
Steelworkers Trilogy, 116–18
Strikebreaking, 41, 44–45
Strikes, 3, 36, 40, 42, 44, 46, 61, 69, 72, 124; corporate campaign and, 46; economic conditions and, 109–10; economic versus unfair labor practice, 45, 48; firm performance and, 75, 77–78, 86, 133; no-strike clause and, 118–19; public employees and, 70; wildcat, 36, 78, 102

Teamsters (International Brotherhood of Teamsters), 49, 57, 69, 112
Textile Workers Union v. Lincoln Mills, 116
Two-tier wage structure, 44, 50–51

Union avoidance, 39–52; communication polices and, 43–44; decentralization of bargaining and, 40–42; industrial relations staff and, 42–43; labor movement's response to, 46–52; profile of union avoider, 45–46; strikebreaking activities and, 44–45
United Auto Workers (UAW), 41–42, 45, 48, 50–51, 54, 56, 121
United Farm Workers (UFW), 68
United Mine Workers (UMW), 57
United Paperworkers International Union v. Misco Inc., 120
United States Department of Labor, 4, 14, 29
United Steelworkers of America (USW), 41, 47–48
United Steelworkers of America v. American Manufacturing Co., 116–17
United Steelworkers of America v. Bethlehem Steel, 115
United Steelworkers of America v. Enterprise Wheel and Car Corp., 117
United Steelworkers of America v. Warrior & Gulf Navigation Co., 117

Vietnam War, 36–37, 110

War Labor Board, 63
Washington Post, 45
Western Airlines, 48
Whipsawing, 40
Work in America Institute, 4
Working-to-rules policy, 47–48

About the Author

MICHAEL J. DUANE is Associate Professor of Management at North Central College, Naperville, Illinois. He has also been Director of the MBA Program at Mercy College of Detroit. His primary publications have been in the area of public-sector labor relations.